DID YOU
LIKE THAT?

DID YOU LIKE THAT?

FRED DIBNAH
IN HIS OWN WORDS

DON HAWORTH

1 3 5 7 9 10 8 6 4 2

First published in 1993 by BBC Enterprises Limited

This edition published in 2009 by BBC Books, an imprint of Ebury Publishing.
A Random House Group Company

The Random House Group Limited Reg. No. 954009

Addresses for companies within the Random House Group can be found at
www.randomhouse.co.uk

A CIP catalogue record for this book is available from the British Library.

ISBN 978 1 846 07637 4

Commissioning editor: Albert DePetrillo
Project editor: Nicholas Payne
Designer: O'Leary & Cooper
Production: David Brimble

Printed and bound in Great Britain by CPI Mackays, Kent, ME5 8TD

To bu books by your favourite authors and register for offers, visit

The Random Forest Stewardship Council (FSC),
the leaing international forest certification organisation. All ur titles
that are prined on Greenpeace approved FSC certified paper carr the FSC logo.
Our paper nvironment

CONTENTS

PREFACE

FRED DIBNAH was born in 1938 into a world which, in his view, has been going downhill ever since.

The high point of civilization had already passed: that was in 1913 when Britain's production of coal and cotton achieved a level never again to be equalled. In summer dawns and in the darkness of winter mornings throngs of workers clattered through the streets to the mills. Everybody had work and money. On the far-flung Empire the sun never set. God, still masculine, was in his heaven. Britannia ruled the waves.

By the time Fred came on the scene at Bolton in Lancashire (he has never recognized the annexation of the town into 'Greater Manchester'), much of the glory and all of the optimism had passed. But the landscape remained: the multi-storeyed spinning mills, the rows of terraced houses and the hundreds of tall chimneys pumping out black smoke that formed a permanent overcast and paled the summer sun.

For young Fred the mills and their machinery and their chimneys with magnificent ornamental tops held an enchantment which he has never outgrown. It is the sad irony of his life that some of the skills he taught himself in the Victorian art of steeplejacking should have been turned to the demolition of what he loved.

The mills have now almost all gone and, looking down from some remaining chimney, he sees in their place housing estates of 'ticky-tacky egg boxes' and windswept industrial estates where 'units with unpronounceable name signs' make flimsy objects or package imported goods.

The Victorian virtues, he thinks, have gone with the mills. People are softer, less knowledgeable, less able, less courteous, less happy. National pride has declined. Social discipline has gone. Fred sums up what he calls, 'the modern world' quite briefly. He says it stinks.

All this, one might think, would leave him down in the mouth, if not ripe for a course of antidepressants, and put him at odds with the world. Not in the least. Life for Fred is essentially a comedy. His own bad times he relates, except in rare moments, as an extended joke. The change and decay in all around him he describes with great regret but also with a certain gleeful relish.

Life is a comedy. It is also an adventure. He is the kind of man around whom things are always happening, and nothing that happens goes untold. The stamina which sustained him for fourteen dogged years in doing up his steam engine can, with sufficient refuelling, carry him through a storytelling marathon until he retires hoarse, or the less wakeful of his hearers slump forward with their heads in the crisps. Nobody has ever complained of getting short change from Fred.

It is fifteen years since we embarked on making our first film together. We have since made a further eighteen. The filming, done at intervals over the years, has been easy and harmonious. Fred doesn't have one face when the camera is running and another when it's not. The only dissension is when we hold back from following him into the detailed technicalities of his craft or go on working too long past the hour of the lunchtime pint.

His first wife Alison and her successor Sue have taken part and put up with us about the place. On our side, the fact that our crew has been small and changed little over the years has helped to strengthen the friendship. Arthur Smith has shot most of the films with his son, Howard, or Dave Horsfield, working at different times as his assistant. Martin Lightening shot the early spectacular scenes from the chimney tops and a couple of the later films. Jack Wilson, our sound recordist until lately, is a trained engineer and struck up a special relationship with Fred by being able to join in twisting knobs and yanking handles on the steamroller in a tutored sort of way. Peter Gibbs and Roy Newton cut the films.

For my part, I cannot claim to have spotted the merit of the subject at first mention. Jean Thompson, research assistant and later associate producer, 'discovered' and recommended Fred. It sounded a bit thin. Climbing up and down chimneys and driving round on a steamroller would hardly stretch to fifty minutes without a very engaging character and a lot of ideas and incident. I asked if Fred could talk.

He held forth for two solid hours at our first meeting and has not dried up to this day. His best tales, which together make up the story of his life, are told in this book.

Don Haworth, 1993

EARLY DAYS

TO HIS mother Fred was always something of a disappointment. She had knocked off work to give birth to him on 28 April 1938, and provided him with the best of starts by naming him after his illustrious uncle Frederick, proprietor of the Temperance Bar in Bolton town centre and purveyor there of hot bitters, a volatile brew, guaranteed non-alcoholic.

Young Fred never looked like rising to uncle Frederick's eminence. Nor did he follow him in his choice of tipple.

At school he was distinguished only by being the pupil at whom the teacher most often shied the wooden-backed board duster. He was an odd sort of boy, a loner. He never played games, but traipsed round after steeplejacks or hung about mills to watch the steam engines and study the machinery.

In Mrs Dibnah's eyes he was headed in the wrong direction. She and her husband had always worked in dirty, noisy factories. She wanted Fred to have a clean-hands job.

For a time it looked as though he might. To her surprise and delight he passed for the art school. But, once there, his dogged persistence in painting only industrial scenes blighted hopes that he might become a Rembrandt, or at least a set designer.

He went to work for an eccentric joiner, learned much and performed well, but caught the artisans' beer and tobacco habit so acutely that when he joined the army his mother felt obliged to send postal subsidies to Germany to keep him slaked and smouldering.

Fred's oddities and shortcomings might have been easier to bear if only knowledge of them could have been confined to a small circle, the family and a few discreet friends. The chimney had destroyed any hope of that.

It was a factory chimney. Fred had erected it on top of his mother's house. It was not big as factory chimneys go but very big indeed for a terraced house. It towered along with Bolton Wanderers' floodlights above the streets. Nobody could miss it.

Through the years Fred had to keep it swept because nobody else would. He used a method he had learned in Germany. Instead of shoving brushes up he worked from the top, dropping down an iron ball with a brush attached.

Mrs Dibnah sat with her memories and her solemn cat opposite the blocked-off fireplace while Fred's ball and brush rattled in the flue.

'He clapped that chimney on the roof when he was sixteen,' she said. 'I've had to live with it ever since. It's awful. I came home one day from work and there it was sticking up in the sky. The photographer came from the *Evening News*. People drove here on Sunday afternoons to stare at it. Everybody said our Fred was a lunatic.'

Fred's boots were heard above. A load of soot huffed down the chimney. Loose bricks fell. The cloth screen at the fireplace puffed and bellied.

'As you know, he went to art school. You'd think he could have got work in an office, a clean-hands job, not doing what he does now. I never thought he'd have been reduced to this sort of thing.'

Fred, for his part, never felt 'reduced' and certainly doesn't now. The most famous steeplejack in Britain, sire of two families, owner and restorer of one stationary and two road-going steam engines, creator of a great steam workshop in a back yard where lesser men might have grown vegetables how could he be thought to be 'reduced' to anything? How could his early days be seen as other than preparation for a grand destiny?

* * *

'We lived first in a terraced house next to a big railway siding. The puffing of shunting engines and the clang of wagon buffers went on all day. At night we slept to the peaceful sound of slowly passing goods trains. Sometimes I woke up and from the bedroom window watched the trains go by. the great monstrous locomotives hauling 50 wagons full of coal. Often the firehole door was open, throwing a great shaft of light into the sky. It caught the fireman and his shovel in silhouette and made steel rods of the pouring rain. A magnificent sight, gone now forever.

'I can't remember when I first noticed steeplejacks. My mother used to say I spotted them from my pram. Certainly when I first went to school I kept a look-out for them from the top of the tram. Little fellows in flat caps or berets, like Tom Thumbs 200 feet up in the sky.

'My early fascination with steeplejacking and steam never diminished. I never really acquired any other interests. Most of my acquaintances have to do with one or the other or both. If, for some catastrophic reason, I couldn't climb chimneys or play with steam engines it would be the end of me.

'My father hated steam. He worked at a bleach works that housed dozens of steam engines driving hundreds of iron pulley wheels and flapping belts. Steam hung about the place and trickled out through the roof slates. The noise of all the gears going round sent people deaf and daft.

'He worked what was called a beetling machine, the ultimate in Victorian engineering. It was driven by its own steam engine and its job was to hammer flat the fibres in cotton cloth. It had a spiral roller like those in vacuum cleaners, turned by iron cogs that revolved through a set of gears that lifted up and down great baulks of timber that hammered the cloth against a wooden beam. It made you think of a xylophone, but its music deafened you for hours afterwards.

'There were no good jobs there. The worst was the job of the oilers and greasers, men who went round with the oil can and kept all the revolving ironmongery lubricated. The death rate amongst them was high as they threaded about the machines and the flapping belts. He came home a few times with a report of another poor oiler caught by his jacket in the works and mangled.

'My father himself worked from seven in the morning until 5.30 in the afternoon. He came home dead beat. The rats used to climb up the spokes and back mudguard of his bike and pinch his lunch out of the saddlebag. He finished up with bronchitis caused by the atmosphere and smoking. It was a terrible place. But it fascinated me, the steam engines and all the ancient machinery. I went down as often as I could in the school holidays. He thought I was off my rocker to spend sunny days in this madhouse of industry.

'He could never really fathom my interests. He never had any money. He was aghast years later when I spent £20 on a motorbike. When I confessed I'd paid £175 for a load of rusty scrap iron in the shape of a steamroller he had to sit down.

'My mother also worked at the bleach works when she was younger and later as a charlady at the gas works. She looked after the pennies. If she found she'd been overcharged she'd insist on going back to the shop straight away. No question of waiting until she was passing next day. She'd go dodging across a field and a busy main road where she might have been run over to get restitution of three halfpence.

'They both had hard lives. He had a long period of suffering with his chest as he got older. His only recreations were acting as a checker on the turnstiles at Bolton Wanderers Football Club on a Saturday and cleaning out his hen pen on Sundays. But it was a comfortable, harmonious home.

'We moved from the house by the railway to the one where I built the factory chimney on the roof. It's still there, incidentally, and public opinion about it seems to have matured with the passing years. I believe there's even talk now of putting a preservation order on it as an historic monument.

'The house was very close to the football ground, which suited my father and younger brother who were fanatical supporters. I never went near but I did make a bob or two out of it storing spectators' bikes in our back yard and on the outhouse roof at threepence a time. At derby games and big cup ties I could make 30 shillings (£1.50) in an afternoon, which was more than a day's wage. We had a tough and often acrimonious time disentangling pedals and spokes in the heap of bicycles.

'I liked the house and I liked the town. In the war years, and for some time after, there was still a lot of manufacturing going on. Black smoke from the chimneys filled the sky. The whole town was covered with settled soot. Even the sheep up on the moors were black. There was a bustle about the place. Factory buzzers sounded, the railway puffed and clanged, people in droves filled the streets going to work. At night they came out through the factory gates like a great swarm of cockroaches.

'I never wanted to go away. I made an annual hullabaloo in defying the do-gooders who ran a trip to Blackpool for children whose parents couldn't afford a week's holiday away. I'd be there in my best gear and they'd try to force me on to the bus. I used to throw one of my wobblers and they had to give up to it. They gave me a good battering and locked me in the bedroom and that'd be the end of it for another year. They all went to Blackpool. I watched the trains through the bedroom window.

'I've never wanted to travel much beyond steam engine range of home. When the army posted me to Germany in my National Service I'd no option. I've never been abroad since for a holiday – which was the issue that finally put paid to my first marriage.

'As a small boy, I used to enjoy going to my grandmother's and building with bars of carbolic soap. The soap was very coarse and in red or green blocks. It came in a wrapper which, I seem to remember, carried a picture of a baby wearing his nappy. We bought it from the Co-op grocery which itself was a wonderful place, very different from the horrible supermarkets that took its place. There was none of the pop music or the wire basket job. The customer was served with some ceremony. Everything was weighed out in paper bags. Potatoes came roaring down a magnificent cloth chute from the roof.

'My grandfather, Albert Travis, had been quite a famous runner back in the early 1900s. I still have a photograph of him in his long shorts surrounded by the cups and shields and canteens of cutlery he won. The photograph is all that's left. Most of his winnings went to pay bills. The doctor, a flexibly minded chap, always willing to be paid in kind, took quite a part of the swag off our hands in payment of his bills.

'By my time, my grandfather's achievements had rather been forgotten and the most prominent of our family was my uncle Frederick, owner of the Temperance Bar. He made his hot bitters in a wooden barrel, stirring the mixture up with a big wooden spoon. It looked like some kind of witchery. I can see him hanging over and stirring, wearing a black apron and a trilby hat with a fag in his mouth with two inches of ash ready to drop from the end.

'Then there'd be a special day, bottling day, when Uncle Edward, who was a signalman on the railway, helped to decant this concoction into bottles. They had a big pan underneath to catch the spillage and, wasting nothing, they'd pour that back into the barrel. Very unhygienic, cobwebs everywhere. They'd crate the bottles and stack them up for the fermentation period. It could be really volatile when they served it, so lively that it could take you half an hour to pour it from the bottle into the pot.

'On Sunday mornings everybody went to Uncle Fred's Temperance Bar and drank a pint or two of this stuff to warm them up for the real thing when the pubs opened at twelve o'clock. It was a billiard hall as well. There was a table in a room upstairs. In those days snooker was rather frowned upon. Proficiency was regarded as a sign of a misspent youth. No longer. It's one way to wealth and fame.

'The best present I ever got as a child was a model steam engine given me by a man, quite an odd ball, who kept birds of many colours. His aviary was close to our hen pen where I used to go mucking out with my father on Sunday mornings. I don't know how it cropped up – I guess my dad must have mentioned to him my disturbing interest in steam – but he invited us to his house and presented me with this beautiful model engine. It stood all of 18 inches high. It had a proper slide valve and a piston, a beautiful brass boiler, pressure gauge, everything. It ran on methylated spirits.

'I spent many happy hours with it until one fatal Sunday night. My mother and dad were in the back kitchen listening to the Palm Court orchestra on the wireless and I was in the parlour running the steam engine on the card table. It was going like billy-o and in an attempt to get even more power out of it, I wedged a dye-cast model telephone box on top of the safety valve, which made it into a potential bomb.

'It went off. The model telephone box shot up like a projectile and stuck in the ceiling, followed by a plume of boiling water which was dripping back down on to the couch and the best shiny table when the door swings open and in comes my mam. I got a real going over. The dent in the ceiling was there for the rest of my mother's life.

'School was always hard going. I was never very academic. Usually I finished third from bottom of the class. The only time I ever shone was when the school was broken into and the burglars made off with all the keys. The headmaster couldn't afford to engage a locksmith for so much work. He was completely stuck. It looked as though all the locked doors would remain closed and all the unlocked doors open in perpetuity. I volunteered to make a complete new set. I'd be about thirteen by then. I knew I could because I'd often watched my dad who was very good at making keys. It was a hobby. I don't know why he took it up; I don't think he ever had any ambition to be a burglar. Anyway I made a complete set for the school. For the only time in my life I was regarded by a schoolmaster as something of a hero.

'Mr Walker was a formidable man, a disciplinarian. He did things they'd never get away with now. He was quick to let fly with the heavy board duster. It flew past 18 inches above your head and hit the wall in a cloud of chalk dust. It kept everybody in line. There was no shenanigans in that class.

'We were made to pay attention by all the teachers. Now children don't seem to be. With all the modern gear in schools they should be cleverer than we were, but it doesn't seem to work like that. They're bigger, but they're not so bright. People's ability to do things has sadly declined.

'I had a friend called Alan Heap. He wasn't brilliant at school either, but we were both industrious at inventing contraptions and attempting minor civil engineering feats. We once dug a tunnel into a hillside on the style of the Great Escape. It was in sand. We shored it up with old picture frames off the tip and pieces of rotting floorboard. How we escaped being buried I don't know. We had a few frightening cave-ins. But we succeeded in driving it 20 yards into the hillside and then we dug a shaft upwards and came out at the top of the hill.

'We made a boat based on a bicycle wheel and some laths stolen from a slater's yard. We had no money for materials but we did have a few tools inherited from my grandfather. The boat sailed all right, but it was highly unstable, like a canoe. You had to sit dead centre. I mastered it to the extent of paddling along the canal to Bury. You had to overcome its idiosyncrasies and a mate of ours paid the price of not having the time to do that. He was keen to have a go, so one lunchtime we got the boat out of the shed, stuck it into the water and pushed him off. I don't know what he did. He must have shuffled about too much. The thing completely overturned and he disappeared under the water, leaving only the cap of his school uniform afloat. He got ashore sodden and shaken.

'We next had a go at making a diving helmet. The basis was a Smiths' potato crisps tin box. We sawed a hole in the front and puttied in a piece of glass so the diver would be able to see out. For the breathing tube we soldered a copper pipe to the top of the box and on that stuck a hosepipe, the other end of which was attached to a lump of cork to keep it afloat. Round the base of the tin box we stretched a motor tyre inner tube which when the thing was worn would cling tightly round the diver's neck.

'I remember lying on the edge of a mill lodge and Alan Heap struggling to shove my head under the surface to test whether the helmet was watertight. The test didn't work. The helmet contained such a large volume of air it was impossible for Alan to thrust my head completely under. It never did get properly tested. The best bet seemed to be the deep end at the local baths, but they saw us coming and barred the way on the spurious grounds that the putty round the glass window would contaminate the water.

'I never learned to swim. I sometimes go cold when I think about those early marine activities. We got fed up of playing with the boat. For a long time it stood propped up and neglected in a comer of the back yard. Then one night a gentleman who passed by regularly on his way to Bolton greyhound racing track spotted it and we did a swop for his Winchester pump-action .22 rifle. It was no good really. It wouldn't work and eventually I swopped it for a percussion cap revolver. At least it stimulated my interest in firearms which became a bit of a hobby. What happened to our unstable boat I don't know.

'These kinds of pastimes and my dismal academic record did nothing to bolster up my mother's hopes for me, but it was actually my interest in steam that got me into the art school. The entrance examination was in three parts. First, you had to draw the usual bunch of flowers, then came the perspective job, then you had a free choice of subject. I drew a steam engine, based on a magnificent traction engine which had belonged to a showman. I had been to the fair every year especially to look at it. One year it had gone, replaced, as all the great showmen's engines were, by a diesel lorry. But by then all the splendid detail of it had sunk into my mind. The drawing got me in.

'I'm glad I went to art school. Drawing makes you more observant. You see things. You notice the detail. You see beauty in all sorts of everyday things that many people overlook. Drawing has also been useful for my business. Not everybody cares for a trip up the ladder to see for themselves what needs doing at the top of the chimney and I can illustrate points in a reasonably clear drawing. That tends to get me jobs in competition with rivals who turn up with a lopsided drawing, nothing in proportion, nothing symmetrical, done on the back of an old piece of wallpaper.

'I soon realized that to get anywhere as an artist you'd got to be brilliant or exceptionally lucky. I was neither. My drawings had a certain style of their own which some people liked and some didn't. I was never very good at drawing people. I stuck to industrial themes – machinery, pithead gear, spinning mills at night with all the lights burning, canal scenes, factory chimneys with scaffolding round the top, landscapes of a world that has disappeared in my lifetime.

'They gave up on me. "You're good with a hammer and chisel," they said. "The best thing you could do is to become a cabinet-maker."

'I was sent to a place down a dark narrow entry, a cabinet-maker's-cum-undertakers. I knocked. The door creaked open. The man behind was pale and gaunt like a corpse. Beyond, in the gloom of the workshop, rows of coffins, beautifully French-polished, stood on trestles. I ran.

'At the Youth Employment Bureau I was met with good tidings. "We've got a good number here with a jobbing joiner."

It was in a posh area of Bolton, Chorley New Road, where all the rich people lived. There were six or seven budding joiners at the bureau after the same job, but I was the only one who went on a bike. I was first to the joiner's yard and I was set on. The boss put me through a bit of an interview, though with the simplest questions. "Do you know what a tenon saw looks like? Have you got a claw hammer?"

'I'm glad I worked for Bill Rawlinson. I was there six years, from sixteen to twenty-two. He was a good craftsman and he taught me a lot. One thing was how to measure. I was never good at arithmetic and I had my own system of measuring. I was more shouted at for my measuring than for any other thing. It made me sharp to spot other people's bad measuring. To this day I'm quick to detect it if those who built a chimney I work on were not too clever with the tape measure.

'Mr Rawlinson had his faults. He easily flew off the handle and he was very parsimonious. He'd brandish a new four-inch paintbrush in our faces. "I've just paid eight and six for this. Take good care of it. Don't leave it out all night so we find it stiff in the morning."

'We tied a label to things he valued. "Sale price 3s 11d." It was a thin joke but it used to drive him insane.

'He ran an old Wolsley Hornet motorcar with a leather body and a soft top so rotted that the rain came straight through. He repaired it by covering it with a layer of shavings, laying a sheet of felt on top of them and then tarring the whole lot as though it was a hencote roof. One morning, on the road to Ashton-under-Lyne, one of the wheels of the trailer he towed came adrift and went bounding past him. He wouldn't pay for a proper repair but he found in a scrapyard some sort of axle with a couple of wheels attached. He left me to figure how to adapt and fit it.

'The car was only used when it was absolutely necessary. To save petrol he sent us out on jobs shoving an old handcart with a wobbly wheel. One Saturday morning an old worker and I set out with two extension ladders and eighteen feet of six-by-four spouting loaded on the handcart. The old chap wasn't in too good condition and he was breathing hard by the time we'd toiled up a big hill.

'"Stop," he gasped. "I must sit down."

'He got his breath back, then went to his tool box, took out his hammer and methodically smashed all the spokes of the dicky wheel. The handcart fell down in a heap.

'He'd had the foresight to stop level with a telephone box. He called the yard. "The handcart wheel's just collapsed, Boss. You'll have to come out with the trailer."

'Mr Rawlinson was always very loath to turn down business, quite rightly, which led to me getting in some useful practice in pointing. A window frame he'd put in needed some mortar work done round it. Neither of us had much experience of that, but I at least had watched it done as part of my steeplejack studies.

'I did that job then, sometime later, a two-week job on a big garden wall, which so pleased the old bird who owned it that she invited us to point the gables of the house. They were three storeys high, so it was a sort of apprentice steeplejacking job. We didn't really have the equipment to work at that height but I made do with Mr Rawlinson's short ladders and bits of boards lashed together. After that we got such a rush of pointing jobs that he added "Property Repairing" to his advertised repertoire and formally permitted me to address him as Bill.

'About this time a friend of mine and I caused a bit of a stir by dangling a dummy from the staging which steeplejacks had rigged up round a 212-foot chimney. We fashioned the body out of wooden laths and fencing wire. The head was a sackful of old rags. We dressed it in some old trousers and my father's boots – filled with concrete so it hung properly – and an enormous overcoat which my friend's wife had inflicted on him from a jumble sale and which he was desperate to get rid of. It's true that few people go up chimneys wearing overcoats but we thought that might be overlooked in the shock of seeing a corpse hanged from the staging.

'Making a start up the chimney carrying the dummy after darkness was quite easy. I climbed on the lee side, out of the strong wind, and in the pleasant light of street lamps and of the multi-storeyed mills which were all then working night shifts. But I climbed on out of the light and into darkness and was hit by the wind the moment I moved round the staging.

'The dummy's legs got wrapped round its head, it spun on its hanging rope, whirled round like a propeller, and fluttered like a flag at ninety degrees to the chimney. Nothing could have been less like a hanged man. I gave up the struggle. I just left it tied there and climbed down and warmed myself up with some fish and chips.

'In the night the wind dropped and a thin fog settled across the town. The dummy hung still. It looked, as we'd meant it to, exactly like a hanged man.

'It was first seen by an old man, an early riser who pulled back his curtains and saw the dreadful spectacle, twisting very slowly in the light breeze. Within minutes the whole neighbourhood had been aroused. The street filled with people. The police and the fire brigade arrived.

'I missed the early fun. I was working at the other side of town and couldn't get across until later in the morning when everybody round there had already been up a long time. Groups of people were still standing about in the street as though there had been some sort of disaster.

'I asked what was going on.

'"Some daft sod hung a dummy from the top of the chimney."

'Everybody, it seemed, had been "dragged out of bed".

'"The mill manager was dragged out of bed," one woman said.

'"Then they dragged the foreman steeplejack out of bed," another woman said. "The police told him he'd have to climb up and retrieve the dead body."

'Before anybody went up some man had the presence of mind to bring a pair of binoculars to bear. He reported a ragbag head, a jumblesale overcoat and a pair of concrete boots.

'But it did come close, as I learned afterwards, to a death in the morning. Sometime later, when I was fitting a new floor, the lady of the house pointed out the chimney as though it was a landmark. "My husband was one of the first to see the figure dangling there. He went down with a heart attack."

'I came over hot and cold.

'"He got over it," she said. "What a heartless, idiotic thing to do."

'It taught me a lesson. I've never done anything quite so foolish since. I was obviously living too confined and humdrum a life but Bill, as I was now privileged to call him, had taken a bit of a shine to me and exerted himself to blow away any notion of leaving. On my long-term ambition to become a steeplejack he made no comment, but he pinned up on an inside door any newspaper report he came across of a fatal accident to a steeplejack. Eventually the door was covered with cuttings like a ghoulish wall newspaper.

'When the time came for National Service the boss did his best to get me off. He got several deferments on the grounds that I couldn't be replaced, but then we had to go in front of a tribunal in Manchester. National Service was coming to an end and if only he could get deferment for another few months I wouldn't need to go at all.

'He was quite eloquent. Six old cronies sat there listening to him. One fell asleep as he sawed on. It did no good. After listening to him pleading for half an hour the chairman said: "We think if you tried you could get another worker like Mr Dibnah. He must go and join the army."

'I had some time to fill in between the tribunal and reporting to the army. I didn't go back to joinering. I did what I wanted to do ever since I was a child. I set up in a small way as a steeplejack. I hadn't many ladders. I didn't get many jobs. I made very little money. But it was a beginning.'

STEEPLEJACKS

'I can't think of any part of my childhood when I was not fascinated by steeplejacks. I'd seen them dancing through the rolling smoke at the chimney top or hanging at the end of a rope in a bosun's chair blowing about like a cork in the wind. On bad days, when everybody in the street below was wet through, steeplejacks went on working on the lee side sheltered by the chimney from the driving rain. If you braved the elements to go back in an hour or two, they'd have completed a new area of beautiful pointing which dried quickly from the warmth of the chimney.

'As a small boy I was intrigued to know how two men, a steeplejack above and his labourer below, could assemble up the side of a chimney all the 16-foot ladders they arrived with. By watching you could learn the principle of the job, but I wanted a lot more explanation of the detail of the art, the trade secrets, as you might say. I was particularly fascinated to watch them at work on ladders fixed to the underside of ornamental overhangs at the chimney's top which they climbed like inverted flies.

'"You need Dak on your boots when you get to there," Harry Holden used to say. Harry was the first among my steeplejack heroes. Dak was some kind of cheap glue manufactured in the thirties.

'I learned, when my time came, that climbing a ladder on the underside of an overhang is the easy part. The difficult part is getting back on to the ladder from the top side. As you approach there's nothing there but the ladder head and a view of the earth 200, or more, feet below. You've got to feel round for the rungs with your feet.

'It was always good fun to watch them getting the scaffolding up, especially when there was enough wind to make the planks dance on the way up. It wasn't difficult to distinguish the good scaffolding jobs from bad ones. The best looked like architects' drawings, the worst as though a biplane had crashed into the chimney top. Either way you'd see them waltzing about on a single plank with the clouds floating by. As a young lad I thought of them as heroes, supermen.

'I used to spy out where interesting jobs were in progress by ascending a colliery slag heap, belonging to the Earl of Bradford, with an old pair of opera glasses. Saturday afternoon or Sunday was the best time when the mills were closed and the soot, settling gently on everything and everybody, left the atmosphere a bit more transparent.

'Steeplejacks, when you saw them on the ground, didn't look like anybody's heroes. They weren't big burly fellows like those you see in pubs these days wearing sweatshirts. A lot of them were wizened, shrunken dwarfs. Most wore berets with a wick on top and bicycle clips to prevent the wind blowing up their trousers. Many of them, you would see as they started up the ladder, had holes in the soles of their boots. They were badly paid and for many what they spent on ale accounted for a fair part of their meagre stipends. But they had a kind of pride about them. They didn't start work and knock off to a buzzer like workers in the mills. They seldom arrived before ten o'clock and they packed up when the mood took them.

'They were aloof. They didn't talk to just anybody. They didn't talk to me. When I asked them questions they waved me away. I doubt if many of them would have been capable of a coherent answer. They knew how to do the job almost from some kind of instinct. Few of them could put it into words.

'I learned quite a lot from watching them, but almost nothing from my attempts to start conversations. I was eighteen before a steeplejack with more in the upper storey than most of them

25

explained the laddering job by drawing diagrams with chalk on the pavement.

'Looking back, I realize I owe a lot to all of them. Even with the best explanations the only way to understand them is by observing, watching very closely what the other fellow does. I don't think anybody could write a textbook about it. There isn't what you might call a literature of chimney climbing.

'Harry Holden was the most distinguished steeplejack working round Bolton, foreman for Faulkners, a big steeplejacking firm from Manchester. He was very smart in appearance, with shiny shoes, a collar and tie and a flat cap and always clean overalls. He was the one I followed round most persistently, though it was many years, and after I'd made a start myself, before I summoned up the courage to speak to him. In later life we became quite friendly. I used to go for a pint with him after he'd retired and he rewarded me with some horrific tales about chimney climbing in the olden days.

'He had to retire early with a chest ailment, the victim, as many of them were, of chimney smoke and Woodbines. I ended up going to his funeral.

'The odd thing about him was that, those few horror stories apart, he was always reluctant to talk about steeplejacking and I discovered that, although he went to a pub every night and played dominoes and cards, the blokes there never knew what he did for a living. He never told them. If asked straight out, he'd say "I'm in the construction industry," as though he were in some way ashamed of being a steeplejack. I could never understand that.

'The old boys, the men who built the chimneys in Victorian times, certainly don't seem to have been ashamed of their work, though they must have been even more badly off than the steeplejacks of my childhood.

'I find their initials and dates cut a hundred years ago in the brick or the ornamental stone at the top of chimneys. There was no practical purpose for these ornamental tops and in my time nearly all mill owners have had them demolished rather than find the funds for preservation. But they were designed and put there, like much in Victorian industry, out of a desire to create something magnificent. Some of the stones weigh 5 tons, hoisted more than 200 feet up by steam power and set by men who, however hard their life, must have had a pride in the job.

'When they finished a chimney it was a fairly common practice to have a roast beef dinner on the top. On the big ones with ledges at the top wide enough to ride a bike round they would hoist up a brass band. Everywhere the Union Jack was flown. It was a time of pride, in the job, in industry, in Britain and its far-flung empire. We led the world.

'I often think I was born out of my time, that I should have been living a century ago. I know about the social horrors of Victorian life but when I look at the beautiful things they made – chimneys, steam engines, buildings – I can't believe that these were created by people who were sick at heart. In many ways it's been decline ever since.

'Alongside the initials cut in the stone of a chimney top are more recent initials of those who, through the years, have gone up to do repairs. The first ones are beautiful, cut with serifs, almost as good as a gravestone. By 1914 the lettering has lost a bit of character and quality, by 1940 it's rough, by 1970 unreadable and by 1980 about as good as small children's graffiti. One letter is 3 inches tall, the next is 2 inches and the one after topples over sideways. How can a man do anything reasonably straight if that's the best he can do with simple letters?

'I think the best time to have lived would have been in the early years of this century when our country was still on the crest of the wave. By the 1930s, my parents' time, industry was run down and many of the mills were decrepit and dreary. But in my grandparents' working years they were beautiful places. They had lovely lodges and lily ponds and handsome cobblestone roads. The master lived in a big house on the hill. He knew his workers and they often addressed each other by Christian name.

'These boss families were in the main hard-headed, clear-sighted people but it's surprising how many of them bred some kind of imbecile, an idiot son, a bad one in the litter, as you might say. They weren't perhaps complete idiots, but a bit queer, odd, AC-DC types. They weren't allowed to stay round to get in the way. The old man would decide, "He's no good for industry" and pack him off to university or to live in the country.

'I suppose for the workers it was quite a hard time but, as a lot of industries have discovered, where there's no discipline they go bankrupt. I've often been in works where I've wondered how they manage to stay in business. There are half a dozen people here leaning on a machine and talking and another group there having a talk and a smoke. Nobody's really working. Production might be ticking over but only just. What pleasure or pride can there be in a job like that?

'I never knew the legendary big bosses in the steeplejacking business. In my early time Faulkner of Manchester was the king of Lancashire. An army of steeplejacks worked for him on contracts covering hundreds of chimneys. He deservedly had a high reputation and is reputed to have made a fortune. He lived in grand style at Nether Alderley in Cheshire and spoke with an Oxbridge accent.

'Earlier, there was the famous Mr Smith of Rochdale who, I believe, had his own carriage on the Lancashire and Yorkshire railway. And then at Oldham there was a man called Ball who lived in a mock castle, part of which still exists. I forget what it was called, not Ball's Hall, but something like that. He went bankrupt, not through the steeplejack job, but because of the expense of constantly restocking a zoo he built. He kept on importing animals that the foul polluted atmosphere kept polishing off. The smoke won. He died a poor man.

'As I get older I sometimes find myself wondering what happens to old steeplejacks. You don't seem to meet many retired ones.

'When I first started I'd quite often find a ragbone man with his handcart of rags and rubbing stones waiting for me at the bottom of the chimney. He'd ask me a question or two and then say, "I used to be in the steeplejacking game."

'Several lay in wait for me. They all said that. I can't believe it was a conspiracy of ragbone men determined to undermine my morale. God preserve me, I thought, from finishing up like that. It was an odd sort of thing to happen but it long ago ceased to worry me. I can't end up like that because there are no ragbone men left. They've disappeared with their rubbing stones from the face of the earth.

'I know of one poor chap whose career in steeplejacking was prematurely cut off. His dad who owned the company ran off with a bird to Blackpool and took all the ladders but one with him. This chap couldn't afford another set and he was reduced to repairing property, pointing round old girls' windows, cutting out woodworm, which he could reach with his one remaining ladder.

'Not many steeplejacks close their careers by falling off. One of the daft questions I'm asked, usually by older schoolchildren, is: "Have you ever fallen off a chimney?"

'I explain that's a thing you only do once, and it's half a day out with the undertaker.

'But quite recently a steeplejack I know did survive a fall. One day when I rang him up his daughter answered the 'phone and said he was in hospital. I asked what was the matter with him. "He's fallen off a chimney," she said.

'I assumed she must have been misinformed. If he'd fallen off a chimney he wouldn't be in hospital; he'd be in a wooden overcoat. But it was true. The chimney he had fallen off was only 60 feet, which is not high as chimneys go but very high as falls go. He suffered a fair amount of damage, six broken ribs, a dislocated leg and other injuries. As his wife said, he'd reorganized his bone structure.

'By the time Sue and I went to see him in hospital he was inclined to laugh off his brush with death. But that proved more painful than the fall. Laughing put him through agonies with his broken ribs.

'The side of the job I'm least happy about, but best known for, is felling chimneys. "Aren't you the chap who topples the chimneys?" people ask me. I am, but I wish I weren't. I'd have been happier if Lancashire was still covered by its forest of chimneys and if I could have spent my life keeping them beautiful and in good nick. I learned felling as I learned other aspects of the job by watching. It's not done by dynamite. Dynamite is all right if the chimney is standing in the middle of a wide open space and it doesn't matter which way it falls or how far the bricks fly. There is seldom that leeway. Mills were built in areas of high population density and quite often there's only a narrow gap between still-standing property to drop the chimney into.

'There is only one accurate method – with the sticks and the fire. The feller, using these days a pneumatic drill, hacks out courses of brickwork at the foot of the chimney at the side to which he intends it to fall, shoring up the gap with pit props as he goes. At completion the gap will be about a metre deep and extend half way round the chimney. A bonfire of old wood and usually motor tyres is lighted against the pit props. They burn away. The chimney falls into its determined space.

'If, of course, all goes well – which it doesn't always.

'I used to go round telling people that this was an old Victorian method, but I recently discovered it's much older than that. The ancient Greeks used it. Attacking a city, they tunnelled under its walls, supporting the tunnel roof with props, then lit a fire in the tunnel and retired to a safe distance. The props burned away and down came the wall.

'I think that's what happened at the battle of Jericho. It wasn't Joshua's horn that tumbled the walls. He was smart enough to take the credit by sounding a blast at the moment the last of the props burned away.

'There's some sort of survival of the horn stunt. Most steeplejacks give an audible warning of the imminent collapse of the chimney. I carry an old fashioned motor horn slung across my chest but quite often in the excitement of the moment I forget to peep it.

'The felling must be partly learned by observation, though when I was a small boy the mass slaughter of the spinning mills had not begun and there were not many chimney fellings to watch. Some of the men doing them were a bit short of practice.

'The first I went to was a sad disappointment. When I was seven or eight the headmaster, after morning prayers, lined us up to march out to the Rose Queen field, so called because the Rose Queen was crowned there at some sort of carnival.

'We sat there in rows all morning. Little men busied themselves round the base of the chimney but nothing happened. We went home for dinner. When we got back the chimney had gone. A spine of thousands of bricks stretched along the ground.

'I didn't learn much from that, nor from the next a year or two later. That was at the Bolton greyhound racing track and I had a grandstand view of it from my father's hen pen next door. It was quite tight. The chimney had to be brought down within the enclosure of the track and away from buildings – kennels, the stand and the restaurant.

'They got the wrong men for it, some wild characters from up in the hills near Nelson. They had no compressor or anything. They just sailed into the base of the chimney with chisels and crowbars and not surprisingly it took them a lot longer than they'd expected. The chimney was supposed to come down at two o'clock in the afternoon. It was winter. They were still frantically thumping away and racing about when darkness fell. Some of the track lights were switched on.

It was nine o'clock when they began to start the fire. It seemed to me, child as I was, that the gap they cut at the chimney base wasn't nearly wide enough. It wasn't either. The chimney, instead of pitching in the desired direction, leaned and twisted and then came thundering down. It chopped the comer off the restaurant and went straight through the dog kennels.

'It's a job you perfect by experience. I had one or two close shaves myself in the learning process. I've done scores now without killing or injuring anybody and with small damage to property but I'm always nervous as the appointed hour approaches. There are days of tension.'

IN THE ARMY

'After the medical officer pronounced me fit to be a member of Her Majesty's armed forces I was shown a seat across the blanketed table from a fat sergeant who would decide what I was actually fit to do.

'"Right," he said, "we've got two good jobs here, the Medical Corps or the Catering Corps."

'I nearly fainted. I know everybody's got to eat and everybody needs mending, but I was the last man for either job. I'd worked outside all my life and those jobs couldn't be regarded as other than indoor occupations. I pleaded with him: "Give me a job repairing tanks or something like that and I'll work really well for you." He drew on his fag and wrote me down for the Catering Corps.

'I did the usual six weeks' square-bashing at Aldershot. It was a hard time. I'd never been away from my mother, and with sergeants threatening to break your heart, most of us were edgy and scared, easily straightened out and made into soldiers. The ones that thought they could beat the army were losers from the start. We left them sweeping up leaves in a blinding blizzard while we moved on to Catterick to learn the basic art of cooking – such things as how to fry a dozen eggs at once and wait till they've all turned plastic before you issue them to the lads.

'There were forty men on my course and none of us had any experience of cooking. One had worked a steam hammer in Sheffield. Several had been bricklayers and there were a couple of joiners besides myself. The nearest to the food business was a chap who'd kept a knacker's yard.

'An old lag advised me to volunteer to serve in some distant spot such as Singapore where the rules were not so severely enforced as at Catterick. I didn't get to Singapore, but I did succeed in getting a posting to Germany. In six weeks I'd wangled my way out of the cookhouse and I never went back again until almost the end of my service. I was with the 14/20th King's Hussars, a posh tank regiment, and I spent my military service in looking after their horses and hounds.

'They had bought a farmhouse within the perimeter of the camp fence but it was almost a total wreck and they needed somebody to do it up fit to stable the horses and kennel the twenty-odd foxhounds that they'd inherited when the 1st Tank Regiment left. I made known my many qualifications as a property repairer to Captain Vivian Jasper Tubbs and was keenly questioned on site by him and Major Faro-Tomlin. They entrusted me with the repair of the high-pitched roof and then with building brick stalls for the horses.

'I didn't fancy going back into the cookhouse with its mountains of potatoes full of eyes and the legions of cockroaches that swarmed from under the doors and hung in the curtains, so I proposed a big digging job at the kennels. Horses and dogs do a lot of peeing and it was all getting sloppy underfoot. What was needed was some sort of drain and cesspit. I took the job on and to make it last I dug what amounted to a mineshaft. It was about 35 feet deep and 4 foot square.

'It was an easy job because the subsoil was sand, easily hauled out in a bucket. But they were very impressed and I was employed for most of my service as a jobbing builder round the kennels and the mess and a keeper of horses and hounds.

'I was quite at home with the building side of the job, but I've never been particularly close to animals, certainly nothing as ferocious as those hounds. When I went into their compound they seemed to think I was part of their dinner. I realized I'd have to get on top of them but I'd no idea how. Then fortunately, I ran across a man who was a hound expert and he told me what to do: "Take in a pitch fork and lay the handle across the first hound that comes for you. He'll see sense and so will the others."

'I tried it and it worked, though there was an unpleasant moment when a big powerful animal challenged me, showing his bared fangs to the prongs of my pitch fork before he backed down.

'They were always hungry. Tons of pigs' feet and intestines were brought in from German butchers in dustbins and it was my job to stuff this messy offal and a stiffening of army biscuits into a field boiler. I suppose you could only look on this aspect as being a demotion – I dropped down from cooking for the troops to being a dog cook. But in general the job was quite agreeable. The only threat of it coming to an end was a regular depletion in the pack of hounds. I don't think the officers were too skilled in handling them because every time they went out they came back two or three short. I was sent out into the forest with a hunting horn to sound, in a forlorn effort to round up the stragglers. Next thing a curious German gamekeeper would sail up on his moped carrying a three-barrel gun and hold forth in an incomprehensible mixture of German and funny English. We came to suspect that what he was confessing was that he'd bumped off another of our dogs. It was severely borne in on him that it would have to stop.

'Without the dogs I could have found myself back in the cookhouse. I was desperate not to lose my job which, apart from anything else, was ideally located. By the kennels there was a hole in the wire perimeter fence and a pub opposite. Nobody could ask for more.

'The job was by no means too demanding once the building work was done and to pass the time I made my first weathercock out of an aluminium tray. To supplement the dogs' diet I used to get bins of leftovers from the cookhouse and quite often the troops had thrown in knives and forks and the odd tray along with the remains of their dinner.

'The weathercock turned out quite well for a first attempt and I was emboldened to mount it on top of the kennels. The officers when they spotted it were quite pleased – which was a relief to me. You never knew in the army how anything would be taken or who was going to jump on you next. Not a bad thing though. If National Service had been kept going it might well have fired all our present vandals and hooligans into line.

'The peaceful tenor of our life was rudely interrupted by a mid-winter exercise on Lüneburg Heath. The (aptly named) Cold War was in progress and the general view was that if it came to a "hot war" battles would have to be fought in the bitter conditions that put paid to Napoleon's and Hitler's ambitions in Russia. The aim was to prove ourselves and our tanks.

'The air temperature was a long way below zero. Lüneburg Heath has a surface of fallen pine needles about 3 feet deep with a subsoil of sand. In wet weather the mulch of pine needles becomes quite spongy and a tank going through squeezes two beautiful grooves. In winter it freezes hard as stone with an aggregate of pine needles embedded in the ice, a nearly impossible surface for tanks.

'We travelled in a Bedford wagon loaded with eggs and bacon and crates of beer. I've never been so cold in my life. The beer froze in the bottles and the eggs froze solid. You could throw them at trees and they bounced off like golf balls. Whisky had no warmth or tingle in it. Drinking it neat out of the bottle was just like drinking cold water.

'None of the tanks got where they were going. The track pins broke. It was so cold that the metal snapped. They were all immobilized. We were all very glad to get back to our horses and hounds.

'In moments of boredom I took to art again. I was very interested in small arms and I made some careful drawings of them which I put up on the wall by my bed space without the slightest inkling of what I was letting myself in for.

'I went down with a dose of 'flu, so bad I thought I was dying. They packed me off to a military hospital and when I started to revive I passed the time by drawing some more firearms, which prompted the Cornish bloke in the next bed to tell me he had a Luger automatic pistol bought from a German. He was in the 1st Tanks. He said all the officers were keen to buy it, but for some reason he wasn't inclined to sell it to them. However he did need money. He was trying to raise £200 to buy himself out of the army. He asked if I'd give him a tenner for the gun.

'Ten pounds was quite a substantial sum to a soldier at that time. The pay was something like 30-odd shillings a week, so little that my mother had to subsidize me with postal orders to keep me in beer money. But somehow I got £10 together and bought the Luger. Under army regulations it should have been kept in the armoury. You could draw it out to clean it but it was an offence to have ammunition. Nine millimetre ammunition wasn't hard to get hold of if you knew where to look. So I kept the pistol in my locker and, for a special treat, took it out from time to time and had a blast with it down at the kennels.

'One day I was lying smoking on my bed, thinking about home and chimneys, when the building shook with marching footsteps and in strode a Military Police sergeant, straight as a brush, medal ribbons spread across his chest, closely followed by a lance corporal with a pencil and board at the ready.

'"We have received information that you are in possession of an automatic pistol."

'If I had any thought of denying it, it was immediately put out of my head by the MP sergeant looking round with some amazement at all the gun drawings on display round my bed.

'Left, right, left, right, left – I was marched up in front of the adjutant, Major Faro-Tomlin. The sergeant with one finger hooked through the trigger guard displayed the incriminating pistol as though I'd shot somebody with it.

'After he'd barked out the evidence the major dismissed him and the other MP and we were able to relax a bit. Thanks,

I think, to my work with the horses and hounds I got off lightly. But that wasn't the end of the hassle. I came to suspect that the MPs' "information" had come through some of the officers in the 1st Tanks getting a grip on the Cornish lad and demanding to know what he'd done with the pistol. It was of the quite rare 1914 vintage, better made and engineered than those of Hitler's time, and it wasn't long before my own officers started to make offers. I remember them advising me at an all-ranks dance not to attempt to smuggle it back to England with the assurance that they'd take it off my hands for more than I paid.

'If they hadn't have mentioned it, it might never have occurred to me to open my career as a smuggler. Passing my tranquil days with horses and hounds, I thought up a grand plan to smuggle it back home in bits. All it needed was a few blokes to take a bit each when they went on leave.

'It's amazing how all your friends disappear when you ask them to do something risky. Nobody wanted to know except a country lad from Derbyshire called Balderstone who was a bit braver than the rest and who was going on leave a fortnight before me. He took the butt. I had the barrel, the breach block and the magazine.

'In those days there were no metal detectors at customs. It was just a matter of looking the officer straight in the eye and saying: "No. I have nothing to declare but a pile of chisels made for me by a German blacksmith."

'I was shocked when I arrived home to find that the butt hadn't arrived from Balderstone. It transpired that when he reached home in the wilds of Derbyshire he'd lost my address. With some resourcefulness he wrote to our pals in Germany for it, but then discovered it himself, written down on the back of his identity card. He posted the butt on to me and it arrived on the very last day of my leave. I screwed the pistol together, fired it in the coal shed, cleaned it, popped it up on the shelf and caught the bus for Manchester to fly back to Germany.

'Eventually, after I was demobbed, I sold the pistol to a police sergeant. I was convinced he wasn't an *agent provocateur* because he came round bristling with all sorts of ancient illegal weapons. He kept mithering. I needed money to tax my motorbike and in a moment of weakness I sold it him for what I'd given, a tenner.'

FRED CAME back from the army aged 24, just before Christmas 1962. He was determined to revive the steeplejacking business he had just about managed to get started in the months between going for his army medical examination and being called up.

That brief venture had been quite encouraging. He had got together some tackle, a few ladders and ropes and planks, bought with money he earned pointing houses at £20 a time, and he had got a base to operate from – part of a decorator's yard freed for his use in return for building a brick wall to replace the rotted fence round the yard.

It cost nothing to live in those early years. Fred boarded free at home. The only problem was to land commissions for jobs: 'I was too young. I didn't talk right. Half the chimney owners I went to see looked round for the exit as though they were confronted by a lunatic.'

Then on to the scene, in a timely entrance, stole Mr Lonsdale Bonner, Fred's old master at the art school.

'He wanted to help me. He was hard up too. So he also wanted to help himself. He thought he knew how to approach the men with the jobs. That was just what was needed. I knew where there were chimney jobs that needed doing. I told him: "For every one you can get me, I'll give you ten pounds."

'He talked posh. He had a Jaguar motorcar. He put a lot of effort into it and in no time he landed me the job of painting a big iron chimney at a well-known cough medicine manufacturers. He got me two more jobs which I finished before my marching orders arrived.'

That bit of success proved to be something of a false dawn. Much had changed by the time Fred got back from the army. Together with the deferments his joinering boss had won him, which made him late in going off to do his two years of National Service, and because the army was short of men as National Service came to an end, he had to serve for a further six months.

Now, at 24, he was rather too old to return to living off his mother. All he possessed was his Luger pistol, a 1927 AJS motorbike in bad condition bought for £20, and the ladders, planks and ropes he had stored away. Mr Lonsdale Bonner was no longer available to drive round negotiating for jobs and a recession had set in:

'To survive I had to take on little property repairing jobs, of which there always seemed to be many, however bad times might have been. Three slates at one place, a chimney pot somewhere else. I've still got the order book. It's incredible how small the bills were – £3 10s here and a fiver there.

'I reckoned that when I got up to £25 I'd earned enough to pay my mam my lodging money and to see myself right for the rest of the week for ale and cigarettes. I'd then take a couple of days out to go canvassing for jobs, knocking on chimney owners' doors. I was more confident about approaching people in authority then, having served in the army under upper-crust officers, and I had photographs to show of the jobs I'd done before I joined up. But they were little jobs, far from impressive. I was unknown. And all the potential customers were strapped for cash.

'In six months I didn't get a single chimney job. Then I took one on for nothing, just for the sake of landing the job. It was at an old brewery. I put a new iron band round the top of the chimney and a new lightning conductor and I painted all the iron bands from top to bottom, all for £45. It just about covered the materials. But I thought it would be something visible to refer to, something that might look impressive enough to get me other jobs.

'It did, but in an indirect way. The man who made me the iron band for the chimney top happened to be talking to the vicar of Bolton, Canon Norburn, who mentioned that his weather vanes at the Parish Church were in a bad way. He gave him my name and the vicar summoned me by telephone. I put on my best suit and set out, quaking in my shoes. The vicar had the highest church tower in Bolton and he was himself a man of awesome presence. He was tall, and he wore a slightly mad expression and a long black frock.

'I feared for a moment that I'd done the wrong thing in going on my 1927 motorbike which was my only form of transport. Far from it. The bike did the trick. His eyes widened. He was over the moon. He confessed to being a fellow vintage vehicle addict. He trundled out his 1929 Humber motorcar, a beautiful antique with a bonnet about 6 feet long and wire wheels.

'It turned out that he was a firearms fanatic as well, a grand collector of weapons, an odd hobby perhaps for a Christian. In subsequent months he made several polite attempts to get my Luger pistol off me and we had a very pleasant afternoon together up on the moors letting fly with all the weapons.

'The job of mending the weather vanes he gave me on the spot. They hadn't been done since well before the war, and they'd gone green and rickety.

'It was a much bigger undertaking than you'd think. From the ground 200 feet below they looked quite slight. It was a surprise to find that the main part was as big as a house door. How the Victorian workmen manhandled them up in the first place I shall never know.

'When I'd repaired the vanes and finished them with gold leaf they were quite beautiful, twinkling away high above the town. They were the most conspicuous advert I could have had and the job put me well in with the clergy. Seeing how well things had gone at the Parish Church I could waltz in to all the other vicars confident that they'd let me have a do at their lesser spires.

'Praise God from whom all blessings flow. I've never had to go knocking on doors for work since then.

'Within a few years I'd achieved the height of my ambition which was to work on our magnificent town hall, resplendently built in happier days with the money cotton made.

'I enjoyed working there, making my inspections by swinging past the clock face on my bosun's chair high above the pedestrians in the town hall square. The job propelled me into a useful sideline, the stone-cutting business.

'Some of their balustrades were in a bad way and they didn't have the funds to buy new shaped pillars at market prices. So I said I'd have a go at making some in my back-yard workshop which was then quite small and sparsely equipped. But I did have a cutter and I made a lash-up to drive it with an old washing machine motor. I thoroughly expected that when I switched on it'd go "ping, ping, ping" and the cutter would shatter. But it didn't. It cut beautifully, just as though it was going through cheese. I was so elated when the stone started to take shape that I went down to the pub to celebrate and I'm afraid I wasn't able to resume that day. But I went out first thing the next morning and made a pillar in an hour and a half.

'That was the first. I've since made scores, and now I've got the proper equipment for stone work. One of my proudest possessions is a big stone saw which runs with a high-pitched musical scream and throws out as it cuts an iridescent fantail of the water run in as a coolant. It's more beautiful in fact than the town hall fountains.'

TOPPLING THE GIANTS

IT HAS been Fred's sad fate that his fame should rest on his prowess as a feller of chimneys. His other work, of maintenance and preservation, passes unnoticed. His fellings attract watchers these days in the numbers of a small football crowd. Year by year he has helped to flatten the urban landscape he enjoyed as a child and still cherishes in memory.

But since the chimneys must go, Fred takes a pride in the precise and dramatic way in which they are laid low. A reluctant executioner, he aims for the dignity of a clean end.

Through the week he drills out the brickwork halfway round the base of the chimney, shoring up the gap with pit props. The felling usually happens on a Sunday morning. Lorries roll up and tip loads of scrap timber and worn-out motor tyres. Little bands of people arrive and help Fred to heap the tyres and timber against the pit props. There are women amongst them. Some are dressed in boilersuits and caps like engine drivers used to wear.

Who are they?

'Chimney enthusiasts,' Fred says.

Nobody seems to know anything else about them. They are never invited. They always turn up. They are dedicated pyre builders.

At the surrounding houses the police go from door to door, evacuating residents and leading them through the streets to a safe distance marked by white tapes strung between lamp posts. Nobody seems to protest. They lock and leave their homes, carrying cats and birdcages, leading dogs and children, pushing prams and wheelchairs. They stop behind the tape and wait solemnly to see what happens.

'He's never had one go wrong,' the contractor assures them. 'There's no danger.'

It must pass through their minds that if there's no danger there's no need to be standing there roped off at the end of an empty street. But nobody makes the point. Chimney fellings seem to enjoy the unopposable status of something between an act of God and a constitutional right.

There is usually a clear area where the mill has been demolished and where with skill and good luck the chimney may fall without spoiling anybody's Sunday by coming down on top of them or wrecking their homes.

The 'chimney enthusiasts' have by now heaped the timber and tyres against the pit props in the chimney bottom. They stuff in paper and douse it with paraffin or diesel oil, then unrequested retire into the crowd, not to be seen again until the next chimney felling.

In the old days the presiding steeplejack wore a top hat for the ceremony. Fred insists on his cloth cap but he carries his ancient motor horn to honk as a final warning when the chimney is about to fall, and most times there is a ceremonial lighting, usually by a woman who is given the honour of striking the match and thrusting the blazing torch into the heaped bonfire.

She goes. Fred is alone. The fire takes hold. There is nothing more he can do. Smoke rolls up the chimney. Flames dance from the top. The burning pit props wilt and collapse. The unsupported chimney falls in the chosen direction.

That is the theory. But much can go wrong. There is always the danger of undetectable weak places in the chimney which can slew it off its line. More often than not there are buildings within range if it falls the wrong way. It's the only job he does that keeps Fred awake at night:

'The insurance men don't help my confidence. They think, "Who the hell is this fellow with the flat cap? He'll do something daft. He'll drop it on top of the mill. He'll bury a row of houses under it."

'Big mill owners also get the wind up. At places where I could fell a chimney into the space between buildings they lose their nerve and want it dismantled brick by brick which is a heart-breaking sort of job to toil at for weeks on end, looking down on to a big area of open ground where I could easily have dropped it in less than a tenth of the time.

'We pull their legs sometimes. At one works, at Prescot on Merseyside, the managing director kept an anxious eye on us as we prepared a chimney for felling in his yard. He was nervous from the beginning. We finished our preparations one morning and we were going to light the fire and drop it in the afternoon.

'I went off for a pint at midday leaving my assistant, Donald Paiton, at the chimney. The managing director walked past looking worried once or twice, then he went up to him and asked: "Do they ever go wrong?"

'"One in four goes wrong," Donald said, "and we've just done three good 'uns."

'There are some hidden dangers, it must be confessed. You don't know what's been done to the chimney over the years. It was a regular practice when a chimney took to leaning a bit to chop out several courses of brick on one side, so it rocked back into true. Then again some of the bricks may have gone rotten. I've come across some with the consistency of cheese.

'We've had some close shaves. One I did at Lancaster demolished a row of greenhouses and put an enormous hole in the wall of the mill. Fortunately the mill belonged to the man who owned the chimney so he took it in reasonably good part.

'Another time on instinct I got the police to shift onlookers from one side of the street to the other, which was just as well because they'd have got a good peppering with flying bricks if they'd stayed where they were.

'I've never killed anybody, nor even put anybody in hospital. But it's always a worry. Some years ago, I was doing one that I had to drop into a 60-foot gap between buildings. I was very anxious about it. I couldn't get it off my mind at night. Then when I was having my tea in the kitchen this item came on the television news in the next room: "Here's one that went wrong.

'Somehow or another I knew it was something in the chimney line. I ran into the front room just in time to see this factory chimney go straight through the middle of the mill, chopped the mill in half that had just been kitted out for three-shift working. Somewhere in Yorkshire.

'How do you suppose I felt after that? They'd had a whole field to get it in. I'd got to get mine down that 60-foot slot. From that day to the Sunday that we did it my nervous system wasn't too good. There are no brave men. A man who says he's brave is either an idiot or a liar.

'My main competition is the dynamite men. It takes me a week to get the chimney ready. They can come along and drop it for a quarter of the money in half a day, which is good enough at places where it doesn't matter where the chimney falls.

'I've known instances in my earlier days where I've wanted a few hundred pounds to do the job and men have come and done it for twenty-five quid, mad men, no pit props, no dynamite, nothing. just chopped the bottom out as though it was a tree. They don't know to an hour when it's going to go. They just keep bashing at it and when it's really creaking and groaning they run away at great speed. All you need is a sledgehammer and a bit of lunacy and you're in business.

'It's a rough game. The 'phone'll ring. Joe Suchabody, demolition contractor, somebody you've never heard of. You go out maybe 20 miles to his site. He'll argue like hell about the price for dropping the chimney, then say, "Right the job's yours."

'Then at night the 'phone goes. 'Joe Suchabody here. I've had somebody round who'll do it for half your price. Ta-ta."

'I put no faith in any deal unless it's written down in black and white and even then it can't be relied on. I've gone with a written order driving round and round unable to find a chimney. Then I've discovered why. It's there but it's not sticking up. It's on the ground. Somebody else has done it and they forgot to tell me.

'Then come the insurance men. They'll send some little lad from their office who's never seen a chimney fall. He's got to work out all the risks involved. By the time it gets back to HQ it could have been Groucho Marx who's knocking the thing down – which upsets me a bit when I think of all the ones that I've done that have gone OK and yet the premiums keep going up and up.

'I've nearly given up insurance altogether for the felling jobs. If there's nothing in the way I'll take it on my own back and good luck to those men. They've got big Jaguar cars and pinstripe suits. What have I got? A second-hand old army Landrover that I can just about manage to keep going.

'All the same, it's not a side of the job I'd want to give up, nor a method I'd want to change. There are few of us left now in the business of dropping chimneys with the pit props and the big fire like they did in Victorian times. I prefer it because it's more spectacular, there's a bit of build-up to it. With dynamite it's only a question of pressing a plunger – boom, that's it, it's all over.

'You've not really done so much. You've destroyed something that took a few men a long time to erect and a lot of hard sweat and labour and when they finished it off they hoisted the Union Jack, no doubt. And you've just blown it up in an instant by pressing a button. If you do it the old way, starting by hacking your way through 3 feet of brickwork at the bottom with a few hundred tons of chimney bricks squeezing on it, at least it's not died too easily.

'I've done some fellings that haven't been too good for the nervous system. One was in a howling gale and I went ahead with it against my better judgment. I'd invited the borough engineer to light the fire in order to make the peace after getting on the wrong side of him.

'What had happened was that the council had contracted me to demolish two chimneys. The first was only 19 feet from a main railway line and the contract stipulated that it should be dismantled brick by brick. That would have been several weeks' monotonous work with a hammer and chisel. I'd just done a highly successful felling which buoyed up my confidence and, looking at the chimney, I saw it leaned away from the railway track. I had no doubt that I could fell it that way without any risk whatever to the railway.

'We did it in the quiet of an early Bank Holiday Sunday morning. Ken Devine, friend, violinist and chimney enthusiast, now sadly departed, got together a small reliable band including his father. We were on site at 6.00 a.m. and the chimney was down at 8.30 a.m. without a brick anywhere near the railway. It seemed a perfect job done in perfect discretion.

'But we'd been spotted. I got a stiff letter from the council accusing me of violating the contract. I would therefore not be paid for the job and the contract for the second chimney, which I would have been permitted to fell, would be withdrawn. I sought the advice of influential people belonging to the local great and good. They recommended a humble contrite approach. I wrote in my best art school copperplate requesting an interview.

'All the right was on their side. I had signed a contract to dismantle the chimney brick by brick. Instead I had felled it and with an attempt at secrecy. They gave me a rough passage. I offered to fell the second chimney free of charge if they'd pay me for the first which, after all, was safely down. It was an economy for them. They seemed interested, especially the borough engineer. "And you, sir," I said, "if you care to come along, can light the fire yourself." The atmosphere brightened. He accepted the offer.

'So when he turned up I felt obliged to go ahead in spite of the howling gale. Everything went wrong. The force of the wind swept the flames away sideways and set fire to the dry grass of an adjoining field, but the chimney itself didn't draw. The props slowly burned away. The chimney should have gone down. But it didn't. It stayed up and rocked in the wind. It swayed three feet out of plumb and rocked back upright. If I'd been told this tale I would never have believed that it was possible for a structure that big to rock so far without falling.

'It rocked back and forth, back and forth. The borough engineer and the spectators retreated to a great distance, having by now no confidence that it would go the right way. In the end there was only one thing for it. We put our 50-ton hydraulic jack in the base at the back and heaved it over. The distant spectators gave a ragged cheer.

'In the above case, the town hall people acted quite well, but in my general experience in recent years their involved regulations and their habitual caution have made life harder for tradesmen like me. Sometimes it costs more time and trouble than the job is worth.

'The first job on which Donald Paiton acted as my assistant was at a new 200-foot chimney built at a municipal incineration plant. It was put up presumably with all the expertise of twentieth-century technology but within two years it was cracked all the way up on both sides. Smoke was issuing from it 60 feet below the top.

'I was called in to ladder the chimney and make an inspection. I took a camera up and ran off three rolls of film which when it was developed caused great excitement and alarm.

'I was asked to send my 108 photographs to a firm of consultants. They wrote back and asked for seven sets. What they did with those 756 pictures I never found out. But you have to humour such people.

'The trouble is you have to humour more and more of them as time goes by. It's no longer simply a matter of sizing up a job, agreeing on a price and getting it done. There are layers of people, all with some bit of authority, to get through – factory owners, property developers, council men, consultants. Factory owners are always skint, developers are after quick money, council people are expert in covering themselves, and the consultants have it made.

'It can't have been like that in Victorian times, or they'd never have accomplished what they did. Even in the span of my career the complications and delays caused by officialdom and bureaucracy have become steadily worse.

'Really, at all chimney fellings there's a conflict of interest between me and the spectators. They all come to see a disaster and it's up to me to make sure there isn't going to be one. I can go through some anxious moments but the danger and the excitement of it are something I couldn't do without.

'I can't think of any better way of getting drunk than after you've knocked a great big chimney down and everything's gone beautifully. It's fallen the right way, nobody's been hurt, you've not done any damage, and when you think what could have happened, what could have gone wrong, the sense of relief is ecstasy.

'Even so, I wish the chimneys didn't have to go. I'd have been a much happier man if the cotton industry had thrived as it did in my childhood days, during and just after the Second World War. I remember as a little lad the magic of riding along the canal towpath on my bike and coming upon a mill of many storeys with all the lights on and down at the bottom this magnificent monster of a steam engine turning a giant flywheel.

It's amazing these days how many people, supposed to be educated, holding a good job and driving a swanky car, just don't understand steam engines. They're totally ignorant of how they work. I accept that everybody doesn't want to know about steam engines but really, when you think about it, it was the steam engine that made Britain great. Now the engines are all gone, the engine room is empty, all the windows of the mill are broken. They send for the demolition men to finish off the mills and for me to destroy the chimneys. At one time they stuck up as thick as blades of grass. Now you can almost count them on one hand, monuments to the Dark Ages.'

BY THE late 1970s Fred had survived in the steeplejacking game for some fifteen years. He hadn't made a fortune; his only vehicle was an old Landrover that had served the army since D-Day and Fred since he had a quiff. But he'd lived and supported a young family and an old steamroller (of which more later) and he had work for a couple of years or more ahead.

He never considered taking on another permanent steeplejack and nobody came asking. Fred was too clearly one of nature's one-man bands. But he has had a succession of assistants, the longest-serving of whom was the late Donald Paiton, a one-time builder, then in his sixties. He was a humorous, sardonic man, sparing in speech and with a sharp intelligence buffed up by a grammar school education.

Working at the foot of the chimney he had an easy command of the logistics of hoisting in the right order the planks, ropes, iron hooks, paint, etc, up to Fred 200 feet above. He saw through con men and charlatans. He saw off salesmen and bores. As a teetotaller he discouraged lunchtime drinking and precarious afternoons. The business was sound. Work was harmonious, though most of the jobs were not for repair but for demolition.

In the summer and autumn of 1978 Fred was demolishing the chimney at the Briar mill at Shaw, Lancashire. Because of the close proximity of other buildings the chimney could not be felled but had to be dismantled brick by brick.

Inside the chimney near the bottom they wedged steel plates inclined towards a hatch cut out of the brick of the chimney wall. Fred, working at the top with hammer, chisel and crowbar, knocked the loosened bricks down the inside of the chimney. They bounced on the steel plate and out through the hatch.

Donald, choosing his moments, kept the hatch clear. A pile of bricks grew at the foot. Gradually the chimney shortened. The demolition stretched out over five months. Hammering week after week alone up in the sky, Fred had a long time to think about the way his job had worked out. He said at the time:

'Steeplejacking suits me because basically I'm lazy and this is an easy-going occupation. When I was a lad I used to see the old-timers stop for a smoke with their knee hooked round a rung when they'd got a hundred feet up the ladders. Now I'm over forty myself, I know what it's all about. When I go all the way up without a breather I arrive at the top blowing like an old steam engine with my heart trying to pound through my ribcage.

'I didn't really want this job so far from home. When I came to look it was a bitter cold morning with the wind howling down from the Pennines. I thought, why do they always send for me at spots like this' I pitched the price high, £7,000 to take the whole lot down a brick at a time, 20,000 bricks.

'I thought that would be the end of it, but they honoured me by giving me the job, which can only mean the other fellows wanted a lot more.

'The weather has barely let up since we came. It's either been blowing a force nine gale or raining or snowing or freezing cold. Up here you suffer. Some days, though, it can be foggy on the ground but quite beautiful up above. You set off up the ladder and climb up through the fog into pure blue sky and the warmth of the sun. The fog lies like a sea with all the chimney stacks and towers and church steeples and the hills outside the town sticking up through it into the sunshine.

'The hot days of summer are best when everybody down below is sweating away indoors and you're alone up here enjoying a nice cool breeze. It's grand to sit on the scaffolding, back to the chimney, looking out. You feel, to be just suspended in the air 200 feet up, as though you're looking down from heaven. You can feel the chimney at your back sway in the wind. They all do, just 2 or 3 inches normally. Then comes a big gust. You feel it sway over, then there's a lull in the wind and back it comes. It's not a lot, but you have the feeling of something pleasantly not quite right, as though you've had five pints of beer.

'At the top of a chimney you have the world at your feet. It gives a wonderful feeling of freedom, as though you're the king of the castle. You get ideas of grandeur looking down at all those humble rows of little houses and their occupants who go through the doors at the same time each day to some monotonous fixed-time job, instead of being up here as free as a bird.

'I'm lucky in the excitement and variety of in my life. Most people have no excitements at work unless they're having a strike. If I was tied to a desk in an office, or a machine in a factory, I'd be watching the clock all day waiting for the time when I could escape. People ask me if I'm not bored knocking bricks off a chimney top all day. I'm not. The job's reasonably simple, so you can carry on doing it without thought. One part of your mind is watching the safety part and the other you can let wander away to more pleasant things like mending steam engines. I've solved many problems while I've been sitting for a breather at the top of factory chimneys.

'You can get a bit lonely working up here all day with nobody but the birds to talk to. I think one reason why I talk so much on the ground is in compensation for my years of Trappist silence on the top of chimneys. I do have a friend who occasionally visits me, Ken Devine who's a violinist in the Halle orchestra. He has a shin up for a bit of a chat.

'Lately though, I haven't seen much of him. His wife found out he'd been coming. She found a photograph he'd taken up here looking back down the ladders and she recognized the toe caps of his shoes which he'd accidentally included at the edge of the frame. She's curtailed his visits, which is a pity. Quite often he brought his violin up and we enjoyed a sort of cultural soirée while I knocked off the bricks.

'But it's grand up here. I always feel well. The height must do something for you. I can go home at teatime and demolish a great lump of steak and a plate of chips. If you're mucking about pointing round somebody's window frames or jobs like that, you get fed up. There's nothing exciting, nothing to battle with. If I don't have any jobs up ladders for a fortnight or so I get all grumpy and despondent. I get thinking that nobody wants me any more. I've got to go and have a climb up something.

'It's a strange job. You become addicted to it. And I suppose you develop marked traits, a noticeable sort of individuality. I know some people call me a nutter or a crank. It doesn't bother me. You can get away with a lot of things that you wouldn't get away with if you were a normal type of person.

'The job does give you a certain pride. An old boy of about eighty who came round talking to me the other day said he used to be in this game and he produced a big brown envelope full of pictures of himself working on chimneys in the 1930s, mending some and knocking others down, same as I do now. They were beautiful. Now in the 1930s life was a bit drab and the average bloke didn't bother to take any pictures of the work he was doing. But this man did because of a sort of love of the job.

'It's an exciting and varied life. You're not ruled by the clock. We don't really have to work at all, not every day. It's like being very rich. You can do what you want. You can take a couple of days off and go and play with your steam engine.

'I was always impressed in the days when everybody else had been working from eight o'clock in the morning to see the old steeplejacks come sauntering up to make a start at about ten and stop for a breather and a smoke after climbing the first hundred feet of the ladder. On very wet or windy days some of them didn't turn up at all. They'd look out of the bedroom window and if the wind was sufficient to raise the underside of the leaves they'd get back into bed again. I proceed on similar lines. Donald comes round at quarter to nine and we have a confab on the weather. If it's bad and the forecast is bad we don't come out to the chimney. We find something else to do, go out to the shed and do a bit more on the steam engine or find somebody's chimney to sweep.

'People say about steeplejacks, "He was always drunk when he went up." I wouldn't say that I've ever done it drunk but a few pints don't do any harm. And Donald, my assistant down at the bottom, is a teetotaller, so on this job we haven't had any pop at dinnertime. I go down to eat my cheese sandwich and to hear his tales of strange characters who always seem to be passing. One day some clown asked, "Has he ever fallen off?"

'"Only once." Donald said, "but I caught him."

'It's essential to have below a steady man with some grey matter. A young lad wouldn't do. He might be good enough at hauling up the planks, but he'd spot some young girl in the office and he'd have gone wandering off when you looked for him.

'I can depend on Donald to anticipate what I want sent up and in what order without having to tell him. Once I'm a few feet up we can't hear each other anyway and it's got to work by sign language and Donald's knowledge of the job. I can depend on him to do nothing rash. Here he's built that massive bank of bricks from what I've dropped down the chimney. I can depend on him to do that and to unblock the chute when it becomes jammed with bricks without incurring unnecessary risks. It is inherently dangerous standing for months on end at the bottom of a chimney that's being knocked down from the top. I watch out for him and he watches out for himself. One flying brick at the back of the neck and he's dead.

'Donald is very inventive. He's found a way round the calamity of me dropping my cigarettes when I'm 200 feet up. It's easily done. You bend down and out sails a twenty packet from your top pocket. You watch it floating down, more often than not straight into a puddle or the mill lodge. I have a distress signal, meaning "cigarettes". Donald hauls some up neatly tied in the rope. It's the matches that usually cause the problem; it's not unusual for them to strike themselves on the chimney on the way up.

'I wouldn't ever dream of going all the way down to the bottom and back just for cigarettes, but I do like to smoke up the chimney – to celebrate when things are going well and to calm nerves when they're not. Either way you don't get much of a smoke on a windy day. The end glows like a welding iron and a whole cigarette's gone in three puffs. I do think a lot about giving up smoking. I know what it did to my father and I know that I'm going the same way. He got bronchitis and coughed himself away. Smoking is a hazard, but then so is climbing chimneys. I would think that if you're very careful and reasonably sober climbing chimneys you'd have more chance of living a bit longer if you didn't smoke. All the old steeplejacks smoked Park Drive or Woodbines – though it's true, they've all gone now.

'One day when I was working at the top I noticed a smartly dressed character with a big black car hanging about down below. When I got down at lunchtime I asked Donald what he'd wanted.

'"He seemed to have a special interest in you," Donald said. "He left his card."

'The card said: Suchabody Undertaker. And he'd written in ink, "Ten per cent discount".

'Really you are dicing with death working on the rotten old top of a chimney. There were some bad ones built in the 1860s and 1870s with ornate tops that have eroded away from the inside, leaving some 8 or 9 tons of coping stone held on just by pure weight and maybe ironwork which was put up fifty years ago to stop the movement but which is now rotting itself.

'I've been on chimneys where my chisel has gone straight through rotten brickwork, making a hole, beyond which there's nothing but the sky and green grass fields and the waves on the mill lodge. I went up one that hadn't been scaled for fifty or sixty years. What had once been the ornamental top was literally just a loose pile of rocks, all lifting up with the movement of the chimney in the wind and shaking about. I got hold of the uppermost stones and they just came away in my hand. Looking down the chimney I could see the inside of the walls all green. Pigeons were fluttering about. One mistake in places like that and it's half a day out with the undertaker.

'Some chimneys are nice and friendly. Some are bad. You know instantly which way it's going to be. I suppose it's the way a climber might feel about different rock faces.

'Up most chimneys there's not a lot of danger unless you do something rash like leaning back levering on a big crowbar.

'I've had few real calamities while working at the top of chimneys. One was letting slip a load of bricks which fell on top of a blacksmith's shop and demolished it completely. I thought, "That's the end of my steeplejacking career." When I got down I was shaking all over and had to go into the pub for a pint. But Mr Courtauld decided that what I'd wrecked wasn't worth keeping anyway and there was only a small claim on the insurance.

'On another occasion I put a rather large dent in the top of a new motorcar. It was parked where it shouldn't have been within the guard rope I'd put up round the foot of the chimney. It wasn't really my fault. I picked up two bricks and the wind whisked off a chunk of mortar which went down like a helicopter on the wind and shattered on the top of a brand new Volvo.

'Another time, I accidentally bombarded a mill office from the top of a chimney. The job was the same as this one here:

to take some height off the top by knocking off the bricks a few at a time. One morning I arrived in dense fog at the foot of the chimney with a cautious old chap called Joe Robinson who was my assistant then. He was appalled when I moved towards the ladder.

'"You're surely not going to throw off bricks when you can't see where they're falling?"

'I needed to press on with the job, so I asked him to make an exclusion zone by roping off an area to one side of the chimney to keep people out of the firing line.

'I climbed up through the fog into brilliant sunshine. It was warm. The birds were singing. The fog lay across the landscape like a white blanket, penetrated by chimneys and church steeples. I had a fag on. The bricks were coming off beautifully. I was humming happily, at peace with the world.

'You get used to the sound that bricks make when they crash down into the yard below. The sound seemed to change. I paused, dropped another brick and listened. From far down below I heard breaking glass, followed by screams of terror and cries of distress and protest. Without noticing I'd worked my way round the chimney top and I was throwing my bricks, not into the roped-off landing area but through the roof of a magnificent office on the other side. I thought I'd killed somebody. I went down the ladders three rungs at a time. Thankfully nobody was hurt but everybody from the mill owner down was covered in plaster. Some cowered in the shelter of doorways, as though from an air raid. Nobody said a word as I inspected the damage. It had been a magnificent office. Now the skylights were shattered and the slates broken. Some cornice mouldings had been brought down and roof plaster lay across everything. Desks, ledgers, typewriters and tea cups were covered in it. The office workers used to change their shoes at work and now they stood shaking with their outdoor shoes in their hands full of fallen plaster.

'Everybody survived but the mill didn't. Eventually it went the way of all the others. It was a beautiful place with fancy gates and a yard of cobblestones, four big boilers, a great big steam engine that drove all the machinery, and fine oak panelling in the offices I damaged. I was then taking 150 feet off the top of the chimney. Years later the mill was demolished and I felled what remained of the chimney. It can be a sad business.

'One bright note though: when I went back for the felling some of the people who used to work in the office came round to see me. They bore no malice. Rather they looked back on the bombardment as an exciting and uniting adventure – as though we'd all been through the Battle of the Somme together.

'Over the years I've had very few accidents and I don't carry more insurance than I have to. I'm obliged to have third-party insurance for people like Courtaulds. If I kill one of their operatives I'm in dire trouble. They'd commandeer my steam engine or something like that. But I don't have any life insurance on myself. It's like being a motorcar racer or this fellow who jumps over cliffs on his motorbike. I'll bet he's not got a life insurance policy. If he had it would cost him a fortune.

'I don't really bother with that side. I'm not going to die, not for a long time. And when I go I'll go with my boots on.'

RUNAWAY WEDDING

'YOU SEE a lot from the peaceful top of a chimney,' Fred said, 'the comings and goings of the frantic world below. I've seen the atmosphere cleared by the Clean Air Act and the distant moors come into view. I've seen the destruction of the industrial landscape and the building of motorways and multi-storey car parks. Through the years I've seen old Nat Lofthouse leading the Bolton Wanderers footballers on cross-country runs and still, well into middle age, leaving the young lads straggling behind. It was from a chimney top that I spotted Alison.'

'He could tell me what time I went to school,' Alison said, 'and later what time I went to work. He noticed the clothes I used to wear. We didn't speak, though. We didn't know each other.'

'Then one night,' Fred said, 'she came into the pub where I was propping the bar up. I'd had a few pints and worked up a bit of Dutch courage. I went over and asked her if she fancied a night out.'

'I was in there with my father,' Alison explained. 'We were on our way out when Fred got hold of my hand and said: "What are you doing tomorrow night?" My dad shouted from the door, "Come on." Fred said, "Quick, where and when?" And I said, "Top of our street, seven o'clock."'

'Six weeks later Fred and a friend took me to a house in Manchester without explaining why. A man there went to a safe and got out a big case of rings. Fred said, "Pick one, we're getting engaged tonight."'

The story of their runaway wedding in May 1967 and of the acquisition back home of a quaint old gate house to live in became during the seventeen years the marriage lasted one of Fred's great set pieces.

'We had a lot of mickey taken out of us because I'm ten years older than Alison. Then there was some bickering about the wedding. Her lot wanted so many coming and our lot wanted so many. So one night when we'd had a pint or two we decided that we'd run away to Scotland. We could stay with Derek Roscoe, a friend of mine from Bolton who was chauffeur to a rich lady with an estate in Kirkcudbrightshire.

'We packed our bags the night before and hid them in the workshop. I left a note at home, collected the bags and set off for the station. I thought, "There's no way she's going to turn up." But she did. We'd got to carry on then with the thing we'd started. We got off the train at Carlisle, went on to Dumfries in a series of buses, then discovered that we'd lost Derek's address.

'We inquired down a line of buses at Dumfries bus station: did anybody know a chauffeur called Derek Roscoe? We were passed on to the driver of a most ancient Leyland single decker, built about 1928, an antique vintage vehicle it'd be now. But he had good news, "I know the man from Bolton. Get in."

'He drove us out across a black sodden landscape under storm clouds and set us down miles from anywhere half way up a mountain. No bus stop, he just pulled up at the side of the road. He said, "He lives at a farmhouse up there." He nodded to a mountain track disappearing between the trees of a great pine forest. It was pouring with rain.

'We'd been walking some time, carrying the bags, when a Morris Minor with two ladies aboard pulled up beside us. We said we were looking for Derek Roscoe. "I know where he stays," the driver said, "Get in."

'They took us to 'the right farmhouse but the woman there said, "He isn't here any more. He's gone back home to Bolton."

'It was still pouring down. There were no more buses that day. They took pity on us and invited us to stay the night. Alison slept in a big wooden cot, which in the daytime was hinged into the wall, and I slept with the farmer in his bed. He wore a big nightshirt and a hat with a big bobble on top like Rip van Winkle.

'I tried to strike up a conversation with him. I thought steam engines might be a likely subject. He wasn't that well up on them, though he did, on taking thought, know the whereabouts of one or two. There didn't seem much more to be said so we went to sleep.

'Having got so far we couldn't lose face and come home so we decided to press on and get married at Gretna Green. But it's not as easy as that. You had to stay there for twenty-one days before you could be deemed a resident of the area eligible to get married at the registry office. We chose the wrong hotel to pass the time in. The one next door was great. They had a party every night. Ours was a rather miserable place. Out of boredom, having nothing to do for three weeks, I pointed the gable end for them. I thought I might get something knocked off the bill but I didn't. The landlady's husband was a Yorkshireman. He didn't believe in giving owt away

'Then Alison, having had time to think about it and being a bit religious, decided we ought to have a do in a church as well as the registry office. The vicar wasn't too keen. He didn't like people who ran away from home. Alison did the talking. I just stood in the background. Over the mantelpiece hung a great, big, magnificent picture of the Forth bridge. I expressed some admiration of it, which seemed to put us in a better light. His attitude began to change and finally he condescended to do the job. I agreed to point his gable end.

'When the great day arrived he was nowhere to be seen. We waited and waited then at last emboldened ourselves to go and knock on the vicarage door. Nobody answered. We waited and knocked again. Eventually we heard some shuffling in the hall and he unlocked and opened the door. He was in his pyjamas. "I'd forgotten about you," he said. "Hang on." He nipped inside and reappeared with his cassock on and his pyjama legs sticking out of the bottom. And in this rigout he married us.

'Back home we lived quite harmoniously for a few months with my parents, then we had the luck to get the tenancy of the splendid Victorian house which is still my home. It belonged to the Earl of Bradford who owned a lot of property in these parts and was offered by his agent for whom I'd done some jobs. He knew I needed a place with enough ground to park a steamroller.

'The house needed some doing up, but the rent was small, and at the back was a good sized garden, 135 feet long and 70 feet wide, where from the beginning I had visions of putting up an engine shed to house my steamroller and eventually of creating a great steam-driven workshop.

'The house and the garden are on a plateau cut into a steep wooded hillside between the road at the front and the river at the back far below. It is listed in the *Historical Buildings of Bolton* as a single-storey gatehouse. That's what it looks like from the road. But the rooms at either side of the front door are bedrooms. The stairs lead down to the living rooms below. We live semi-subterranean like rabbits. Most people know to come round the back. Fresh visitors who knock at the front door are surprised to be invited down a flight of stone steps as though they were being asked to descend to a cellar.

'When the agent died the estate decided to sell the house and asked for an offer. One day when I returned from work Alison told me she'd offered the person who came round £5,000. I was pretty sure we'd never get it for that. The responsibility for selling it passed, for some reason, to a character at Cambridge who asked if he could come up for a chat and mentioned that he'd like to have a look at my steam engines.

'I thought, "Ah, now then, Cambridge, they're big steam men down there. I'll impress them with my steamroller and get a bit knocked off the price of the house."

'It was raining the day he came up, so Donald and I didn't go to work and we had the steamroller ticking over in the shed when he arrived. He seemed quite impressed. I wandered round the house with him, showing him all the bad points, especially a great nasty bulge in the back wall that could at any time collapse and let the whole lot down into the river. He agreed to £5,000.

'When I looked closely at it, I could see that the back wall really was an urgent job. For a few dreadful minutes I thought I'd left it too late. One morning when I was lying in bed there was a hell of a bang. I thought, "That's it, the back's fallen out." Actually it was a gas explosion. The wife came running upstairs screaming, with no eyebrows and a big hole burned in the front of her dress. The gas cooker had blown up.

'I've done a lot to the place over the years, first to make it safe for another century, then to build on a two-storey extension. As it's a listed building everything had got to look just right. You've got to have old second-hand bricks. After many a month of prowling round old buildings that were about to have the big hammer we came across a row of houses due for demolition in which the bricks in six of them had never been pointed or messed about with in any way. They made a perfect match with the rest of our house. So we went with two Landrovers, Alison, her father, Donald and another lad, and we literally took the front out of the six houses and brought the bricks back to build the extension.

'The window bottoms and the mullions and the window heads are made of old gravestones. The lad who did the drawings for the extension got rather carried away in his use of stone work. Stone is expensive but again we had a windfall. We met a vicar who had modernized his cemetery and had a big heap of old gravestones he didn't know what to do with. He said, "You can have 'em if you'll shift 'em." They were ideal, so we brought them back and sawed them to length and put a bit of a bevel on and they look quite good. I hope we haven't imported any ghosts. I wouldn't want the place to be haunted.

'I also had a stroke of luck in acquiring a big stone ball that sits nicely at the apex of the gable. A friend spotted it in the front garden of a schoolteacher where it was doing no good. It was only a hazard to fall over if he came home drunk at night. We did a deal: he brought his school kids round to see my steam engines in action and we relieved him of his stone ball.

'The big chimney I built on the extension is the second factory-style chimney I've put on top of a house. The first, as you know, was on my mother's house in my early youth. Now there's this one as well, made of stones I rescued from a dismantling job at a Victorian mansion. It's built in the style of the 1870s and there aren't many of the originals left. They've nearly all had the fancy top ripped off if they haven't been demolished completely. When I've gone people will think, "That's a very unusual chimney stack." I suppose you could say it's a memorial to the great age in Lancashire of steam and boilers and spinning mills – and me.

'The house is ideally situated. There are not too many houses close by and most of them have put double-glazing in, so my evening operations in the workshop don't really cause much disturbance, apart perhaps from the reverberations of my steam hammer which Donald said he could feel in his house 200 yards away. I refrain from doing heavy blows after nine o'clock at night.

'The workshop surmounts a wooded bank that drops steeply down to the river. Beyond that lies the cemetery where we shall end up one day. Somewhere in there is the first and, I think, the only man in Bolton to be killed by a lion. It was in the Wakes Week some time in the 1890s. The lion tamer ventured into the cage and, I suppose, provoked the animal, and his attendants stood by with long iron rods which were kept glowing in braziers to drive the lion off if it rounded on him.

'It can easily happen when nothing goes wrong for a long time that people get careless. Somebody forgot to light the braziers, so that when the lion went for him there were no red-hot iron rods to get it off. He ended up here in our cemetery.

'My father used to tell me about a big flood which raised the river swirling above the banks and washed some of the corpses downstream. I don't know what truth there may be in that, but I do know that along the river bed you can still see all sorts of gravestones, swept in perhaps by the flood. When my time comes I don't think I'd find a nicer or more peaceful resting place. It's quiet, they cut the grass regularly. Not that you would notice that when you're 6 feet under, but it's nicer than being roasted in some crematorium and turned into a little plastic bagful of fag ash, isn't it? I wouldn't mind building my own gravestone. I'd make one like a mill chimney with a lightning conductor and a steeplejack's scaffolding up in position and a beautiful fancy top like the ones that almost everywhere now have been demolished.'

WHEN FRED married and left home his mother was relieved of the daily anxiety she felt about the dangers of his job: 'It won't be me any longer watching the clock and worrying when he's late coming home from work. That'll fall on his wife now.'

In the first days Alison kept her imagination in check by staying well away from any chimney where Fred was working. Her anxiety grew after the birth in June 1968 of their first child, Jane. Fred persuaded her that it might be reassuring if she faced her fears by coming to see him at work.

'So I wheeled Jane round in her pushchair,' Alison said. 'I looked up and saw him, a little figure up in the sky. I was frightened to death. I didn't go to another chimney where he was working for a long time after that.'

'There's no need to worry in the ordinary run of things,' Fred said, 'The time to get the wind up is when I have to tackle something specially hazardous, like the rotten old ornamental top of a chimney which when disturbed might come thundering down and take me and the scaffolding with it. Touch wood, that's never happened yet.

'But everyday steeplejacking, climbing ladders and dancing about on the top of chimneys, is pretty safe. Some jobs you can safely do with a few pints of bitter inside you. You're preserved by an unconscious instinct for survival. You know all the time at the back of your mind that if you put one foot wrong you're dead.

'Falling off has never worried me. I never think or even dream about it. I sometimes think about failure of the equipment, like a rope breaking. Whenever I climb into my bosun's chair I give a bounce on the seat to test the rope and I'm ready to grab the ladder. There have been a lot of accidents through failing equipment and collapsing masonry, but just walking off into the blue through sheer negligence is a thing that seldom happens.

'There must always be some danger, but if I worried about it all the time and what might happen to the wife and kids I'd fast become a nervous wreck.'

ALISON LEARNED to take the same attitude. 'I realized that if I sat at home worrying I'd become neurotic and we'd have three neurotic children. You've just got to put it to the back of your mind. I've come to think he's safer up there than he is on the ground sometimes.'

'That's true,' Fred said, 'the only time I've done myself an injury on ladders was when I fell from a pair of steps in the girls' bedroom. I landed on a drilling machine and knocked myself unconscious. The morning after I couldn't get out of bed and I had to stay there for three weeks.'

'There's no living with him when he doesn't have a climbing job in progress,' Alison said. 'He's only happy when he's working up a chimney, particularly if he has a good one to mend. He enjoys that and I'm happier too. I know where he is. He can't get drunk up a chimney or waste time playing with his steam engine or talking which he does so much of.'

'There's nobody to talk to up there except the birds,' Fred agreed. 'You're out of everybody's way. You're unimpeded. You can make a bit of progress.'

Alison said: 'I believe in God and I think if you're good he'll watch over you. Fred's not bad, he doesn't do anything wrong, so I think he should always be all right.'

'Good, clean-living lad,' Fred laughed. 'I've no enemies. I don't know anybody who doesn't like me. Just the odd person, perhaps.'

From the beginning of her time with Fred, Alison had a rival. She tried compromise and protest, understanding and hostility, friendliness and threats. The contest was to go on, blowing hotter and colder, for nearly twenty years. The rival was a 13-ton Aveling and Porter steamroller, built in February 1912, and dumped long ago by the Flintshire county council.

'A lison did actually come with me to bring it back, though we were not yet married at the time. I paid a Welsh scrap merchant £175 for it, thirteen tons of rust really. It was a far cry from the beautiful showmen's traction engines I used to admire as a child but by 1966 when I was looking round there were so few of them left that they cost far more than I could ever hope to find.

'The steamroller I bought was spotted by chance by a farmer who was wandering about an old army camp at Risley near Warrington looking for a lost cow. He happened to peer through the grimy windows of a big ramshackle shed and there among the junk and rubbish stood this old steamroller. It was of especial interest to him because he had an 1899 Foden traction engine and he mentioned his discovery to a neighbouring farmer who knew me and passed on the tidings. One summer evening I went over and we broke in. The steamroller was in a very forlorn state standing there surrounded by broken-down old army lorries. There were patches of green paint still left on it but it was rusted all over and its anatomy riddled with holes. I was highly elated. It looked the style of thing that might be in my price bracket. The next step was to find out who owned it. We scrabbled round among the papers in what had been a bit of an office and found some billheads of a dealer in second-hand commercial vehicles in Flintshire. I wrote off but got no answer, but I couldn't get this old roller out of my mind and I decided to go down to Wales in search of this scrap chap. I found him at the address I'd written to, a broken-down cottage surrounded by clapped out old army lorries piled on top of each other and leaning against the cottage walls. The man came blinking to the door. He apologized for not answering my letter. "It's the wife's job to do letter writing," he said, "and she's been ill. Give me £175 and it's yours."

'I took the precaution of having it looked over by a boiler inspector and accepted for insurance before I handed over the money. I never got a receipt but I don't suppose that after all these years anybody will dispute that it's mine.

'The next thing was to get it home. The farmer who had spotted it, being a steam enthusiast, bent his efforts to the problem. He towed it to his farm where on summer evenings a steam friend of his called Walter Fitter helped me to fettle it up just sufficiently to get it back to Bolton and gave me some lessons in driving it.

'The noise was horrific, like a bucket of spanners being flung around but with ten times the decibels. You couldn't hear yourself think. You were left stone deaf. When I got down and drove the Landrover I couldn't hear the engine at all. It was perfectly silent like a Rolls Royce.

'I think it was these early journeys in the steamroller that caused my present deafness. I'm only deaf in one ear, the left, which is on the flywheel side. I think the racket bounced off the flywheel and hit me in the earhole. I'm all right on the right-hand side.

'It took two trips to make the fifteen miles back to home. Bits were dropping off from the start and we'd only steamed about four miles before we conked out. At this last gasp I jangled off the road into the drive of a market gardener who was good enough to let us leave it there until the next weekend. We put right the offending bit that had let the job down and just about made it home. We stopped, hissing steam, on the cobbles outside our front door. My father emerged into the daylight completely horrified at the sight of this enormous engine towering up to the bedroom windows. He was stunned to hear that I'd spent £175 on what, quite understandably, looked to him like a load of scrap. He thought I'd gone mad, absolutely lunatic. He'd never seen so much money in his life and his only transport, apart from his legs, had been his bike. But as the years rolled by and the engine became shinier and more beautiful, more like the state in which it left the works in 1912, he revised his attitude and began to take some pleasure in it: "This is our Fred's steamroller." A bit proprietorial, very proud.

'It caused quite a stir in the street. The curtains were pulled aside as the neighbours peered out. The kids were fascinated and most of the older folks were understanding or at least tolerant, but one old guy made a pain of himself, and I felt obliged to move it. A friend of mine had promised that if ever I got a steam engine I could park it in his hen pen, but unfortunately he'd died in the meantime. However, the man who had taken the hen pen over agreed to admit our steamroller as though it was an obligation inherited with the hens and the huts. He was, as it happened, the Earl of Bradford's agent who later got me the tenancy of my house. At the hen pen everything went amiably between us. I worked on the engine and he looked after his fowl. Then one Sunday afternoon when he arrived with his bread crusts to feed his geese we had steam up and the guy who was working with me blew the whistle. It frightened the geese to death. They went berserk. They screeched across like a squadron of Lancaster bombers. With commendable restraint he quietly asked me to remove my steamroller. It wasn't unreasonable. These things are not everybody's cup of tea. I found a field not far away where I was allowed to park it, but it was a tedious business because whenever I'd been working on it I had to sheet it up before I went home to prevent kids from climbing over it.

'I didn't make much progress until some time later when the earl's agent got me the house to rent. It was very forgiving of him. I also think he was glad to see me safely quartered at a good distance from his geese.

'The job of restoring the engine went on for fourteen years. My father wasn't quite right in saying it was all rusty. Only the best bits were rusty. The worst you could see daylight through.

'If you've got a pot of gold restoring a steam engine is easy. You can say, "I'll go and see Suchabody at such a big engineering works and get a bit made." But if you don't you've got to fathom the job out so you can do it with the primitive Victorian methods that were used when the old boys first made the engine.

'When I did the firebox I went to the local ironworks and asked the main man, "Have you any good riveters left?"

'He said, "All the good riveters are dead."

'I said, "Well, do you know of any passable ones still living, retired perhaps?"

'He gave me one or two addresses, and I did find one to help. He was getting on in years, a bit shaky, a Capstan full-strength man. He came down and taught me a bit about the job.

'I drilled 232 holes in the firebox with a ratchet drill by hand. I had bottles of Guinness lined up. Vrmm with the drill, take a swig, back and make another hole. With a job of that size and only the evenings to do it in you couldn't afford to keep popping off down to the pub. Once in there the sense of urgency disappears. You get with the lads and you think "Sod the holes. Who wants to go back in the cold working a ratchet drill, drilling holes through inch-thick iron?"

'But a pint or two on site did take some of the pain out of it. You needed to remember to get all the holes marked out right while you were still sober. The drilling itself didn't require quite so high a standard of sobriety. I think a lot of drinking went on in the olden days when work was really hard and strenuous.

'Most engine men are not married. They say the virtue of steam engines is that they don't answer back. You can belt them with the hammer and they say nowt.

'You've really got to be dedicated or a bit crackers to persist with it. Quite a few friends who have started with great enthusiasm and all sorts of shining ambitions have given up broken in health after the first nasty winter. It kills a lot of men off.

'When you do the job yourself you appreciate the suffering of the old lads who used to build steam engines. Poor devils, they worked in sheds with dirt floors smaller than the one in my backyard. At Taskers at Andover they still knocked rivets in by hand in 1917. I've got picture books showing all the lads lined up to have their photo taken with big moustaches and union shirts and hammers on their shoulders, all looking gaunt and white. They made these great powerful engines by hand. They had practically no machinery at all. Everything was hard.

'If you've done it, as I have, virtually the same way as those men did it, you appreciate what they had to do, not only on some evenings, but on every working day of their life. You know why they looked old and died before their time.

'I think about them and I hope in my turn it might confer a certain immortality on me to have resurrected this steamroller from a pile of rust. I've done my best. Everybody in this business tries to do an even better job than the original builders did. I'm sure it's here now to stay. I don't think even the most wicked scrap man would put the burner through it. Some day perhaps it'll be stuffed in some museum or sold to another crank like me. Once you have repaired it you're only looking after it for future generations.

'It must be a form of immortality. When I'm long dead it'll still be here. Even if they drop a nuclear bomb it would blow all the houses down but do no more damage to my roller than tip it over into a ditch.

It could stay there rusting until eventually whoever might be left came round and found it. "Mm," they'd say, "I wonder what men were like when they made these?"

'The job took me so many years for lots of reasons. There were no spare parts for these old wrecks. Anything appertaining to them had long since been thrown away. I spent days prowling round scrapyards, tugging at bits of iron that might be adapted. I didn't have experience; I had to learn the job as I went along. I didn't have the money to pay for big jobs at engineering works; I had to puzzle out how to do things myself and keep what was farmed out down to the minimum. But that was all part of the fun really. I was wrapped up in it. I've spent hours up chimneys of which I can remember nothing because my mind was occupied with thinking out the next job on the engine.

'What held the job up most, I suppose, was that from the time the engine became just about roadworthy we used it for trips in summer so each year I had to put it all together when the daffodils showed through and take it apart again in autumn for another Winter's work. But that again I don't regret. We chuffed off to all the steam rallies within range. We never had any other sort of holiday.

'For family use we needed a living van, equipped with beds and cupboards, to tow behind the roller. I kept my eyes open as I went about and one day I spotted one in the middle of a field of sheep in the hills above Burnley. I was just in the nick of time. The farmer was out. I told the young girl who answered the door that I'd give him £30 if he wanted to sell.

'"I think he might," she said. "He's only going to bum it to recover any scrap metal from it."

'He rang up at night and we settled for £35. Done up, it's worth well over £5,000. But it took a lot of doing up and for a time diverted my efforts from the roller.

'These vans were provided for steamroller drivers when they were working away from home. The roller company imposed strict regulations but with some concessions. The 1933 rule book of the Lancashire Road Roller Company stated: "Under special circumstances no objection will be taken to a man's wife occupying the van for short periods."

'His own wage was sent on for him to collect at a post office near where he was working. It amounted to £2 1s (£2.05) a week, plus a bonus on days he was actually rolling of 1s 6d (7½p) a day, and ninepence (3¾p) for the Saturday half day.

'The van I bought was in a bad way but it was mainly a job of joinery, the trade I'd been apprenticed to. It took a lot of wood. It's hard to believe, seeing it from the outside, but it took a thousand feet of tongue and groove board to make up the sides. I think I made a solid job of it. I parked it on the road outside the house and some midnight maniac under pursuit by the police crashed his van along the side. All it did was to damage three boards on our van, but on his vehicle it ripped off the whole aluminium side which shot out the pop rivets as it sheared away. They peppered our paintwork as though somebody had sprayed it with shotgun pellets. It was soon put right.

'The van is really nothing more than a box on wheels, but you really need one. It's a support vehicle. Steamrollers never needed to have any great range; the tender at the back holds very little coal. But the van has a grand coal compartment, under the bed and accessible from outside, that holds 5 cwt. You've a cupboard in the comer of the van to keep the food, a place to keep your oil can so it doesn't get nicked in the middle of the night – and of course accommodation for all the family as well.'

ON THE ROAD

FROM THE time some twenty years ago when his steamroller became fit to drive on the road Fred took every holiday break at steam rallies, apart from one traumatic week at Blackpool, to which we shall come in due course.

The children of his successive families, the three girls and now the two boys, started their steam career by travelling inside the living van, progressed to sitting, legs dangling, on the front footboard of the van, and graduated to the coal tender of the steamroller itself.

The years of steam journeys outlasted the lifespan of a sharp little mongrel Nickie who travelled, rain or shine, like a mascot on the footboard of the van. She let out a yelping bark, which harmonized with the whistle, whenever they moved off. White by nature, she darkened in the course of a sooty day's travel to matt black and was scrubbed white again when the engine was cleaned and polished at evening.

Travelling at little more than four miles an hour, they were easily outsped by children on bicycles but just about capable of overhauling most pedestrians, especially the aged. For all aboard it was a hard bonejarring ride which, as Fred has often been moved to point out, is inherent in the nature of the vehicle:

'Steamrollers were not built for speeding along roads but for rolling them. They're heavy pieces of industrial machinery, never intended to be a means of transport. They've no springs. Every time you go over a manhole cover it rattles your teeth. A steam tractor, which was out of my price range when I bought the roller, is a different proposition. It's well sprung and it'll romp along at sixteen miles an hour with half the pain.

'We stop frequently at pubs to allow the family to stretch their legs and for me to fortify myself for the next leg of the journey. A pint or two eases the suffering a bit. It begins to feel a lot less bumpy and bangy than when you're stone-cold sober.

'I know of old fellows, over seventy, who the doctors have kept warning, "If you don't get rid of that thing it'll kill you." And often it does. You notice they haven't turned up at a rally and you hear they've gone. "Old Ned's passed on to the other land. Fell off his engine."

'I don't know whether it's done me any great harm, apart from deafening me. I think the oil thrown from the pistons in front of you is more harmful than anything else. It covers your face and clothes in spots and makes your eyes smart. It is one good way, though, of knowing whether the engine's running all right because when the thrown oil changes from warm to red-hot and burns straight through your shirt you know there's some trouble afoot. Some part of the works is getting warmish. My steamroller is reasonably quiet now as these things go. Some have gearing so badly worn that you can hear them from two miles away. In the cab they can't hear a word, however hard they bawl into each other's ear. They have to resort to conversing in sign language as they clatter along. But there's something about any steam engine that gives you a grand feeling of power and importance. People pay hundreds of pounds, don't they, for recordings of a Black Five locomotive pulling forty wagons of coal, and they sit there in raptures listening to the thing toiling up a hill. It's the noise that does it, the rattling and the shaking and the chuff, chuff, chuff.

'We make a lot of stops. Apart from the pubs and stops to hump the coal up from the bunker under the living van bed to the tender, we have to pull up every seven or eight miles to fill up with water, eighty gallons. We steal it from fire hydrants.

The quicker you do it the better. I call on the services of the wife and kids and they've all been very well trained, both broods, in rolling out the hoses and coupling up.

'It is illegal without a licence but the authorities close their eyes to it. Or they did until recently. I heard a distressing tale from the South of England of somebody fined £1,000 for helping himself from hydrants. It struck me as a bit on the top side for a few gallons of water. In my opinion they should pay us an annual fee for testing water hydrants because half of them are not working. If you arrive in the middle of the night with your steam engine and find the hydrant full of mud you can clean it out at your leisure. But suppose the house opposite were burning down, what time would the fire brigade have to dig the dirt out? We've done it for them. We might have averted a great conflagration.

'It's very important with a steam engine not to let the water level fall too low. You could have an explosion that'd wreck half the neighbourhood.

'Steaming along in the countryside we pass some nice big houses. If I played golf and had no interest in steam engines I'd like to live somewhere like that. But you can't have a Victorian steam workshop in the back garden of a £300,000 house. Even where I live there have been murmurs from the neighbours from time to time, but the type of people that buy very expensive houses in the country would be very insistent on peace and tranquillity. They'd be distressed to see a boilermaker's shop take shape in the next back garden.

'I do actually know a fellow who owns one of these posh houses. He used to live near me but made a lot of money and moved out to the country. We sometimes call on him when we're out with the engine, but it nearly always ends as a booze-up which impedes progress and gets us into trouble with the wives.

'A steam engine introduces you to all sorts of strange people. They come to have a look and some of them end up as friends for life. One day we were grovelling at a hydrant in the road to fill the thing up with water when a party of people appeared out of a converted barn, a very swanky place. They inspected the engine, we struck up a friendship and we call there every year.

'Meeting people is really the pleasure. I don't actually care for driving along through the countryside. It becomes boring. One field looks very much like another. I know there are different varieties of trees, oak trees, ash trees, elm trees, but one tree looks very much like another. You can have too many of them. Factory chimneys aren't like that. They're all different.

'What you particularly don't want is too much sunshine. It just doesn't go with driving steamrollers. After a full day's steaming everything in the cab is red hot down to the footplate you're standing on. Your feet are stuck to the bottom of your boots, you're covered with hot oil.

'Rain is better. It cools everything down. The steamroller is covered by a good roof and it's only when you get down for water that you're exposed to the rain. It does make the going a bit trickier. Ascending big hills you've got to watch that the thing doesn't, as we say, lose its feet. A steamroller can easily skid because it has no rubber tyres, just the iron back wheels and the roller at the front. Going down a big hill you must avoid going over a manhole cover with a wheel that's driving the thing, because that will start it sliding and you don't know where you'll end up.

'Evenings are pleasant when it's dry and cool, chuffing along in the setting sun. Motorcars zoom past at high speed. You wonder where they're going in such haste and why the world has got to go so fast when you can travel along in a steam engine. It's a bit bumpy but very peaceful. Sometimes on narrow roads you get a great pile up of vehicles behind the engine and van. Ninety-nine times out of a hundred they bear with you, but occasionally you get some irate bloke hooting his hooter from some way back in the fine. "Let me come by – you've no right on the road with that thing" sort of style. I have a riposte for those men. I wait for them to get level, then blow the whistle. With 200 psi in the boiler ripping through the whistle it nearly blows all their windows out as they zoom by.

'Steam engines are very safe vehicles. I know of only one that might be accused of causing extensive damage. The owner had souped it up, put a bigger sprocket on the engine shaft, so it would do seventy miles an hour. As he came belting over the Pennines on the M62, cinders shooting from his red-hot funnel set fire to a field. The smoke pall from the burning corn caused two or three motor crashes, burned down two electricity poles and cut off the electricity supply to a village. When the police caught up with him miles further on he was astonished to hear of the disasters he'd left in his wake.

'Most of the accidents are not caused by steam engines but by motorcar drivers who have no notion of a steam engine's momentum. You're approaching traffic lights and you start making your preparations to come to a graceful stop when some clown in a fast car cuts in right in front. You can't see him at all from the cab. You have to take drastic action to avoid flattening him into the road – a Casey Jones sort of job: handle back, regulator open, screw on the brakes and hope for the best.

'Other drivers are genuinely interested in steam engines and allow themselves to be distracted. They turn round in the seat as they come by, so they're driving forwards and looking backwards. The most spectacular case of that sort happened when we were en route to somewhere in Cheshire, me and Bill Greenhalgh and another lad whose name I can't remember.

'We'd had nothing to eat since seven o'clock in the morning and at about 1.30 p.m. in the afternoon we passed a shop with beautiful looking pies temptingly lighted in the window. We pulled into a lay-by, went back for the pies and sat out in the sun on the front board of the caravan.

'A big Rover zoomed up at about sixty miles an hour. As it got level with us the driver banged the brakes on and the passenger stuck a camera out of the window to get a shot of the engine. The driver of a car behind them hit his brakes and, skidding sideways, thumped into their car. Then bang, bang, bang, three following cars ran into each other like shunted railway wagons. Out they all got with their insurance documents for a roadside argument, adjourned for some time when drivers in a growing tail-back started honking. The damaged cars were driven up on to the grass verge and the argy-bargy resumed. By this time we'd finished the pies and been round with the oil can and we set off again, running over all the broken chromium strips and light lenses the crash had left in the road. As we passed they stopped their quarrelling and waved us off in a most friendly manner. We were surprised at the time and I've never understood the logic of it since. It wasn't our fault – we were parked off the highway – but indirectly we'd caused about £5,000 worth of damage to their motorcars. It showed good grace to give us such a hearty send-off.

'The nearest I ever came to disaster was one Sunday when I nearly wrecked a geriatric hospital. I had a huge load of stones to deliver to a posh restaurant. They offered me sixty quid and I promised to deliver them with my steamroller. Michael Webber helped me to load up a big trailer. It weighed about three and a half tons and we must have put 20-odd tons of stone on it.

'We set off for the place. It was outside Bolton up on the moors and the road was steep, something like one in seven in places. The engine was working so hard that the heat burned all the paint off the funnel. When we arrived it took us a couple of hours to unload and by then it was going dark. We lit the lamps and set off back down the hill. The crankshaft started to go too fast. We picked up speed. The 3½-ton trailer which had no brakes added to the momentum. I knew that ahead of us in the gathering darkness lay a 45-degree bend. The road was wet. We were doing about twenty-five miles an hour, six times our normal speed. There was no chance of getting round.

'I screwed the brakes on. The driving wheels locked and the engine slewed with its trailer from one side of the wet road to the other.

'I suppose we were in mortal peril but my main concern at the time was that I might damage my paintwork by hitting the stone walls on either side of the road. I told Michael to get in the coal bunker and prepare to bail out. I tried the Casey Jones job, handle back, regulator open. The driving wheels revolved backward but didn't grip. We went on skidding from side to side without losing speed. The bend loomed up ahead. We were never going to get round. Ahead lay a three-foot drop into a field which sloped away steeply. This way we'd either have overturned or careered straight across to the far side where there was a fourteen-foot drop into the back of a geriatric hospital. Almost straight ahead of me at the side of the road I spotted a big stone pillar carrying a No Entry sign. I decided to hit it.

'The pillar shattered into scores of flying pieces. The whole front of the 13-ton engine reared up in the sky. The back wheels stuck against the stump of the pillar. The front end hung for a few seconds in the air, then crashed down, shattering the front forks into three pieces. The boiler gouged a trench in the road eighteen inches deep. The raging fire set the tarmac burning. By great good fortune the chains hung on to the roller. If they'd broken, the roller would have bounded across the field and into the geriatric hospital. It would have been like the Dambusters.

'I once had a close brush with the law in the middle of the night. I was driving the steamroller up a one-way street in the middle of a town in the Pennines, not to mention any names, when I realized I'd run out of fags. Without thinking what I might bring down upon myself, I slowed to a stop and shouted to a policeman in a doorway, "Are there any cigarette machines near here?"

'"Yes," he said, sauntering up, "but they're all back the way you've come."

'We'd been heavily on the pop all weekend and I was well over the limit for driving a steam engine or indeed any kind of vehicle. Moreover, I didn't want the policeman to see what I'd got on the trailer at the back. It was a chap who'd been with me. He was unconscious and lying sheeted up in the canvas we cover the engine with. It looked like a roll of linoleum, except that he was a great big fellow, 6-foot-odd, and his size sixteen boots were sticking out at the end. I didn't want to risk moving the engine forward and, under surveillance, negotiating the oneway system, so I announced that I'd leave the engine and walk back. The policeman came with me. We walked over a hump-backed bridge. I was sufficiently clear in mind to know to say as little as possible, get the cigarettes, and quietly get under way again. But when I got back the engine was surrounded by police cars. There were blue and white 'uns and orange and white 'uns, every kind of police car you could imagine, and seven or eight policemen as well. The chap I had with me who we'd rolled up in the sheet had risen. He was vertical. I thought it'd be, "Who's in charge of this machine? Will you please blow in the bag, sir?"

'I being of low stature, they were all looking down at me. So I gave myself some elevation by getting up to the footplate. Nobody spoke. The only thing I could think to do, to avoid too much talking, was to say, "I'm sorry, gentlemen, I must go. I've got to be back in Bolton before dawn."

'I might have been a bit slurred, but nobody made a move. So I opened the regulator and shoved the handle forward. and away we went chuff chuff, down the road – shadowed by all these police cars. Two miles along we had to stop to take on water. As we were grovelling in the road with the hydrant gear and the hose pipes, the police cars pulled up alongside. The sergeant got out and eyed the engine over. All that came into my head to say was, "Do you like these things?"

'His eyes lit up, they went big – just like a little lad who's seen a wonderful toy. I said, "Would you like a go?"

'His eyes grew even bigger. So I said, "Come up and have a do. You can't drive it but you can steer it. You'd better take your tunic off because it pitches out a lot of oil."

'He gave his tunic to his chauffeur and climbed up. We toiled for about four miles up a big hill. The funnel was red-hot and glowing cinders shot out like Roman candles. Very spectacular. Both of us were covered with oil. When he got down the sun was coming up over the Yorkshire moors. He said with deep feeling, "Thank you very much," and returned to his duties.

'I spent the next two days in bed recovering from the great drinking bout we'd had that weekend and reflecting on my luck. Not many people have been driven home drunk by a police sergeant on a steamroller.'

IN THE whole of Fred's acquaintance only other engine owners have regarded his interest in steam as anything short of excessive. His father, it will be recalled, hated the pounding steam engines in his workplace and feared to see in Fred's boyhood passion for them the symptoms of an unbalanced mind.

In later life Fred's customers despaired of wresting him away from his steam engines. Standing with them at the foot of chimneys he would affably diagnose the problem and agree a price. That might well be the last they would see of him for a long time.

'Fred,' said one, echoing scores, 'we've got the mill right and we must have you to the chimney. It can't wait any longer.'

'Don't worry,' said Fred.

'But I do worry. And I have been kept worrying for a long time.'

'As soon as I get the last brick off where I'm working now I'll come here. I'll not be going anywhere else.'

'Good. When can we expect you?'

'Well now, that's hard to say. We've had heavy weather,

wind, rain, snow, force nine gales, icing. I'm disgusted with myself I should have finished the present job months ago.'

'We must have you here, Fred. It won't wait any longer.'

Of all who knew him, his wife Alison contained her exasperation longest, until the summer of 1985 when her tolerance finally ran out. That was still some years ahead when one day they talked about their life with steam. Fred said:

'Lots of people I've come to know over the years with the chimneys say, "You spend too much time playing with your steam engine. You should come and get our jobs done" – which in some ways is very true. I have neglected my business and, well, everything really for the sake of that 13 tons of iron.

'Steeplejacking is a spasmodic job. You're tempted to play with your steam engine instead of going to work. It's a bit like being very rich. You can have a day off whenever you want.

'That thing and me now, it's a death-do-us-part job. It's caused much upset in the household, complaints of no holidays, divorce proceedings threatened. "You love your steamroller more than you love me" sort of thing, which I think a lot of men who have steam engines will have gone through, especially the one-man-banders who have one engine and one wife and one shed.

'Alison complains that I spend more time in the shed than I do in the house. Sometimes it's three in the morning when I come back across and find she's repaired to bed. But it's better, isn't it, than being down at the pub all night or out womanizing or doing breakings and enterings?

'When we came to christen the roller and it made loads of noise I thought we'd call it Thunderbolt or something like that. Then I thought I might gain a bit of grace by calling it after Alison. I keep telling her, "It's not every woman that has a steam engine named after her."'

Alison accepted the honour but was always worried about the expense. 'Fortunately I've got a good mother and she helped a lot. When we had no money because something had been bought for the engine it was always all right to go and get food off her or she'd fetch me something round. She'd see the kids were all right for their clothes and then my sisters used to send me clothes for them.'

'You've got to have a very good wife that understands you if you have a steam engine,' Fred explained. 'When we were first married things were a bit rough between us as regards the roller, with divorce proceedings imminent on quite a lot of occasions. But as the years roll by I think Alison has got more liking for the thing.'

But steam remained a man's world. 'Very few men with engines are married,' Alison said. 'They just think that women and steam engines don't mix and they tend to look down on any wife that arrives. They suspect that a wife might try to make her husband get rid of his engine – which has been known to happen.'

'That's tragic,' Fred said. 'They're finished. Their eyes go dull. They've no more use for life.'

'There's no way I'd want to get rid of ours,' Alison said. 'We've done without for so many years to get it built up. I couldn't bear to part with it. There's too much of us in it.'

'We have the reputation,' Fred said with some pride, 'of having one of the happiest marriages in the Lancashire Traction Engine club. In practical terms if I fall off a chimney next week Alison has something to sell. It has her name on it. She's learned to drive it.'

'And to keep drunken men off the footplate,' Alison said. 'Before we had the van the engine cab got crowded with drunken men, Fred's cronies. I decided when Lorna was eighteen months old that the choice would have to be made between the drunken men and the children and me. We won. We got rid of them. The girls ended up travelling in the coal tender. It was a victory for family life.'

'I suppose drinking and playing with these things is all very well if you don't do any damage,' Fred said. 'I've heard of lots of instances where they've had too much pop and things have gone hopelessly wrong.'

'It wasn't only drinking,' Alison said. 'As I say, in the early days they just didn't speak to you. You were lucky if your husband came near you because he was off with all the other men.'

'They're all very nice people,' Fred explained, 'but they were sort of—'

'Bachelors,' Alison put in.

'Odd-ball types perhaps,' Fred suggested.

'Like Fred, all a bit eccentric.'

'I'm not odd. There's nowt wrong with me.'

'Just eccentric. If he gets parked outside a pub at night you never know what might happen. One year he stayed late in the pub. I'd got the girls to bed and I was tired so I went to bed myself. About midnight there was a series of bumps and the van rocked and moved. All the cupboard doors flew open. Tins and pots and cutlery flew out. The kids shouted. We'd no idea what was happening to us.

'It seems that after his last pint Fred had decided he didn't want to stay where we were, so he came back to the engine and set off in the middle of the night. Everything was knocked flying when first the engine and then the van went over the edge of the kerb.'

'It was partly the drink, partly boredom,' Fred explained. 'I came to the conclusion, talking with the chap in the pub, that it wasn't a nice place to stay. It was pitch dark, somewhere in the wilds of Cheshire, so I decided just to put another ten miles on. We carried on going until we came back to civilization, the lights on the Chester road.'

Alison returned to the overweening demand the steamroller made on resources. 'Everything has to go on that. When he started to lose his hair he refused to consider diverting any funds to get himself thatched.'

'It was rotten when it first started falling out,' Fred said, 'but you can hardly say I'm one of the best-looking men in the world, so I just stopped worrying about it. Millions of men are bald and there's no way I'd be so vain as to get a hair piece. More than likely when I was up a chimney it'd blow away in the wind.'

'But at the time,' Alison said, 'I think he really was worrying a lot about his hair so I wrote in reply to a newspaper advertisement about hair transplants. A man came round. Fred was upstairs having a wash, and I shouted up, "Come on down. There's somebody to see you." They had a talk, then when money was mentioned Fred took him outside.

'He wanted seven hundred quid for three rows,' Fred said, 'and he figured that in my state I'd need more than three. I took him into the engine shed and showed him the steamroller. It was just at the time that we realized it needed a new firebox. Seven hundred pounds would buy all the materials we needed for the job. So I explained, "I'd sooner have a new firebox in my engine than a nice head of sprouting hair. Thank you. Good night!"'

A VISION OF HEAVEN

'As I've mentioned, I got the big break that launched my career when the Vicar of Bolton let me gild his weather vanes, and I've never looked back as far as vicars are concerned. I enjoy working on churches, especially on spires. Some of them are hard to get up. There are gargoyles and fancy bits sticking out and if you knocked them off in putting the ladders up the vicar wouldn't be very pleased. But at the top, at the slender point of the spire, there's a wonderful feeling of being alone in the sky, as though you're touching the clouds. Especially from the spires of churches built on a hill, you can survey the countryside for miles around and feel like the king of the castle.

'It's nice and peaceful up there with the birds, remote from the world down below where everybody's racing about like lunatics. Sometimes if I'm feeling a bit low it restores serenity. I find myself thinking about the workmen who built the spire and how they must have struggled to get all those big rocks up there.

'In the olden days rich men who wanted to do something for the glory of God struck up a great church spire like the magnificent ones at Salisbury and Lichfield. What the Victorian cotton barons and coal-mine owners did round here in the 1870s and 1880s didn't quite rise to that height. But no doubt they too intended it to be to God's glory. Living in the midst of throngs of poor people, they may all have thought as death approached: "I'd better do something now for mankind; I'll knock up a big church."

'They weren't all bad men. Lots of them built schools and left parks for the public. But they lived on the misery of other people, all those who toiled long hours in the mills or crawled along a two-foot shaft digging coal. The owners lived in luxury in beautiful mansions, the few who made everybody else suffer.

'I'm not a churchgoer but I believe in God. I sometimes think when I'm up a spire that that's the nearest I'll get to him. But I have a feeling he might know me. He might recognize me. "Oh, that's him who climbs up my church spires."

'Alison used to say, "You'll never fall off. There's somebody watching over you." She thought I was actually safer up there because quite often I trip over things when I'm down on the ground. You need somebody to look after you a bit in the steeplejacking job.

'Sometimes I think he doesn't like me when I travel to a chimney and climb up and then the heavens open. I might just as well have stayed in bed. The other day I drove twenty miles to a chimney at Oldham, just got to the top, and I could see it coming. Everything was disappearing about five miles away under an advancing curtain of snow. Up there it doesn't fall straight down, it comes sideways on the wind. You could be as white as a snowman within three minutes. I moved round the lee side, protected by the chimney and watched it hurtling past.

'It's those days that you get a bit upset with that fellow up there. But there are other days when you set off and it's dull and horrible and you think you're going to have a bit of a bad time today and then all of a sudden the sun comes out, or you climb up through the fog, and everything's beautiful. But there are more bad days than good.

'The really upsetting thing is when you've finished a big load of pointing and you're heading home and the rain comes lashing down. You wake up in the morning and you're frightened to go and have a look at what the weather's done to it. But when you get there, more often than not it turns out better than you thought it might. It hasn't done nearly as much damage as you'd prepared yourself for, and that's a mercy.

'The big thing is the Lord has never let me fall off or drop anything and kill somebody. All the same I never make any presumption. Whatever I'm climbing I treat with the greatest respect because I know the thing'll kill me if I don't. I often wonder when I'm working at churches about what happens to you after you're dead. I've never met anybody who's been and come back, but there are a lot of people with more brains than I have who think there is this wonderful place somewhere.

'My idea of heaven would be somewhere where nobody did any fighting, nobody was hungry and there was plenty for everybody. My little bit of it would be to be left alone with a big pile of rusty steam engines and enough iron plate to mend them. It would be quite wonderful. You wouldn't have to worry about where your next dinner was going to come from. You could just get on with mending those ancient relics for ever.

'I like working on churches not least because I'm preserving something, not destroying it. But the church business is getting a bit thin. Religion has run out of money. The old girls, spinsters or widows of cotton families, who used to pop off and leave the church £20,000, all seem to have gone. At one time, if there had been a good will and a large amount left to a church, the vicar was in a position to splash out on a big renovation job. But there aren't those kind of windfalls any more. Most churches are reduced to the cadging job with a lollipop or a thermometer stuck up outside. There are still a few that have some money and provide nice jobs that you can do profitably but in a leisurely and thorough way. But most are quite poor. Even our own parish church in Bolton can't any longer afford gold leaf for the clock face.

'The problem came to light when we were summoned round to unbend the fingers which had got wrapped round each other in a storm. That involves dangling down from the parapet of the tower in my bosun's chair. They asked me while I was up there to inspect the clock face. It was very bad, but they couldn't afford a gold-leaf job, which would have been quite expensive for a face that size. So I volunteered to paint it gold free of charge. I cleaned all the muck off the cast iron, painted it gold and gave it a protective coat of varnish. I hoped it might do them for a few years. It didn't last a month.

'A week or so after we'd done the job, Donald's wife went into town shopping and reported back that the clock face was going black. I thought her eyes must be failing but the next week Donald went into town and confirmed the glum tidings. "It's nearly black, Fred," he said. A couple of days later another chap reported that it was completely black.

'In three weeks it had gone from a beautiful gold to a dirty dark green, if not actually to black. It must have been a chemical reaction between the gold paint and whatever was beneath it, or to the varnish that I put on top. It looked terrible. From the middle of Churchgate you couldn't even tell the time.

'The vicar asked me what could be done. They still couldn't afford gold leaf so all I could think of was to paint it yellow. And that's what we did, gave it a coat of yellow gloss. It's a terrible thing to do, but it doesn't look so bad from a distance. I don't suppose the average person would know.

'At another church I was asked to inspect, the ornamental figures surmounting the tower were about ready to fall into the street and the cast iron ring round the clock face was only held on by rust. The lugs that secured it to the wall had snapped off completely and it could easily have turned a wedding into a funeral. Even if nobody perished, the bride could have finished up with two rings – her wedding ring and the big cast iron one from the clock.

'I get on well with most vicars and some of them have become good friends through the years. They do tend though to be a bit more persistent than industrial customers when they've got a job that wants doing. One of them used to hide behind his lych-gate and fly out, like a pigeon from a steeple louvre, into the path of my Landrover. He once even shot out in front of the steamroller.

'The more moderate vicars restrain themselves to getting into a huff on the telephone. "Where are you? What are you doing? When are you going to come? You've had the job for eighteen months."

'They seem to think you're sitting at home with your hammer in your hand and your ladders lashed to the truck just waiting for them to ring up. It doesn't work like that. They're speaking from the warmth and comfort of their vicarages. They don't seem to understand that I'm at the mercy of the weather. It rains and it blows and it snows and you just can't make steady and uninterrupted progress through a list of jobs.

'A lot of them resort to writing letters. "Dear Mr Dibnah, If you feel you can't get round to doing our job we will get somebody else."

'Nearly always they end up with a bit of a clanger. They'd be better waiting, and biding their time a bit.

'What's the hurry? It may well have been raining in to the church spire for twenty years. The pigeon muck will have built up so much in the bell room that it blocks all the holes where the water should run out. But nobody has been up there to shovel it up. They think it has just started, but really the trouble has been there for donkey's years and they haven't noticed. But most vicars can see the funny side. I've had quite a bit of fun on church jobs. One day I went to rescue a weathercock that had been dislodged by a storm and was dangling down the church spire. The vicar was a budding photographer. He arrived with four cameras hanging round his neck and clicked away taking scores of photos as I got the ladders up the spire.

'Now we'd had a particularly heavy session on the booze the night before and I wasn't feeling too well. As dinnertime approached a painter who was working at the pub opposite shouted up, "Would you like a pint, Fred?"

'It was just what I needed. I came down and the painter approached along the church path with a pint in each hand. I think the vicar took a dim view. He looked a bit uncomfortable but he sat on the wall with us. We were looking up at what I'd been doing up the spire when a woman jumped over the wall with a camera at the ready and said, "Can I take a photograph of you and the vicar?"

'We looked an odd crew, me and the painter with our pints and the vicar with the cameras dangling round his neck. With great presence of mind he leapt for cover behind the gravestones. The painter and I had our photos taken alone.

'At old churches I like to have some time to stroll through the graveyard to read the stones. Some are moving, some are quaint. One that sticks in my mind was to a Victorian coal miner who was killed by a roof fall in a mine. They went to great pains to dig him out, then immediately buried him again in the churchyard. I think that might have amused him.

'But the old gravestones are something else that modernization is destroying. At many places they've pulled out all the gravestones and grassed the ground over for easy mowing. The gravestones are propped up against the boundary wall and often the older ones, which are the more interesting, are smashed up to make fireplaces.

'The most alarming time I've ever had on a church job was at St George's in Bolton where I was on the tower painting the flagpole. The man who had let me into the church and through the tower door said he'd leave the key with an organ repairer who was working there. From time to time, as the day went on, notes of his music floated up to me at the top of the flagpole.

'At knocking off time I went down the spiral staircase. The door at the bottom was locked. I rattled and shouted. Nobody heard me. The organ repairer had done a conscientious job of locking everything up and gone. It was a solid mortice lock, too strong to force without doing a lot of damage. Back I went up the tower and shouted for help over the battlements. Of course nobody could hear me 150 feet below. It was half past five. The traffic was dense and everybody was going home. I made frantic gestures. Nobody saw me. Very few people do actually look above them when they're walking in the street. These days everybody seems to go round with their heads down. It's a sign of the times.

'I was hungry for my tea. I didn't care for the prospect of spending the night sitting on the stone staircase of the tower. But, as I hadn't made myself seen or heard with all my bawling and gesticulating then, what better chance would I have tomorrow? I might never be noticed. They might forget all about me until some distant future time my remains were discovered. And what would Alison think? What would she tell the girls? She'd already be bothered that I wasn't home for tea. What would she think when I hadn't returned by dawn or during the next day or the days that followed? I felt as cut off from mankind, as remote from help, looking down at the people and traffic below as though I'd been in the middle of the Sahara.

'In time the street cleared. A solitary man, who must have had very sharp ears, heard my waning cries and went for the verger and the key. I had in fact been marooned up there for little more than two hours but at the time it seemed like an age. For some reason I can't understand I was more alarmed than I've ever been by real dangers.

'Apart from that one escapade I've always enjoyed the peace of working on churches and for my part I try to work quietly. I only once made an appalling noise. It was at a church where my father was helping me to fit wire netting inside the top of the tower to stop pigeons getting in.

'Towards the end of the morning we heard a shuffling up the spiral staircase and the vicar appeared. There was to be a funeral service at quarter to twelve. Could we suspend the banging? So, on time, we downed tools. Through the louvres we saw the cortege arriving. It was a real posh upmarket job with a Rolls-Royce hearse. The male mourners had black top hats. The vicar was coming up the path, holding the cross aloft and followed by the pall-bearers.

'Looking round I happened to notice that the wire that drove the chiming mechanism of the clock had come off the pulley wheel and was resting on the spindle. To put it back was a little job that could be done quietly. It meant raising a little the big, 2 cwt, cast iron weight that the wire carried, but fortunately that had stopped level with a guard rail that fenced off a wooden shaft in which the weight was suspended. The shaft went down eighty feet into the church.

'We devised a simple lifting mechanism. We got a plank from the comer and placed it under the weight and on top of the guard rail to act as a lever. I told my dad: "You press down on the plank and as the weight goes up I'll put the wire back on the wheel."

'It didn't quite work. We were a bit short of height on the fulcrum. So we searched around in the dried pigeon droppings and found half a brick, which we wedged between the plank and the guard rail. My dad shoved down on his end of the plank, the weight rose a little and I flicked the wire back on to the pulley. Success. "It's on," I said. My dad let go of the plank. The brick fell into the 80-foot shaft.

'Down below, by this time, they were three-quarters of the way up the aisle. The deceased had been a bleach works owner, powerful, trouble at t' mill sort of chap. Our brick shattered the reverential silence, echoing all the way down the shaft, boom, boom, boom, as it fell like something thrown down a mineshaft. We couldn't have made more noise if we'd tried. They were petrified, paralysed with horror. They thought the old bugger had woken up.'

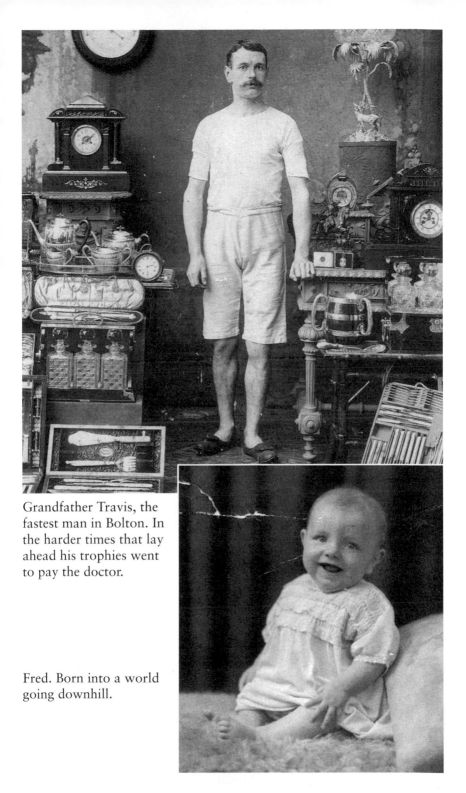

Grandfather Travis, the fastest man in Bolton. In the harder times that lay ahead his trophies went to pay the doctor.

Fred. Born into a world going downhill.

Bolton 1938. 'A bustle about the place. Shunting engines puffed and wagon buffers clanged. Factory buzzers sounded. People in droves filled the streets going to work.'

Fred's first mark on the landscape. Mill chimney on his mother's roof.

Parents. A lifetime of toil.

Laddering – the art that fascinated Fred in childhood. Ladders are hoisted up by rope over a pully on a hook which has been driven into the brickwork. They are secured by lashings of rope to each other and to hooks in the chimney wall. Laddering a chimney is a morning's work.

Dreaming of home and chimneys.

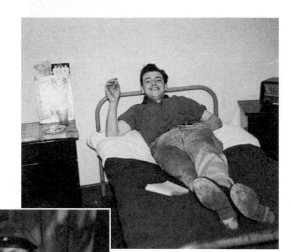

Keeper of the regiment's hounds and horses.

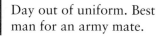

Day out of uniform. Best man for an army mate.

E1927 AJS motorcycle. Won the vicar's heart.

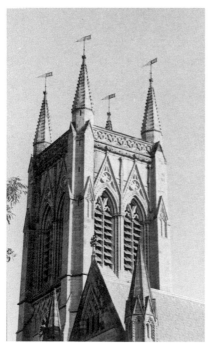

Parish church weather vanes.
The job that launched
a high-level career.

Town Hall. Built by King Cotton,
preserved by Fred Dibnah.

Chimney base chopped out in preparation for toppling.

Stricken giant. Last moments in the life of a chimney. Fred, after many topplings, is still a reluctant executioner.

Donald Paiton, master of chimney logistics.

Tall chimneys, dark skies. The sooty days of childhood.

End of the day.

Married at Gretna Green.

Home. Victorian gatehouse, living quarters below, parking space for steamroller in back garden.

Steamroller young Fred came home with, a rusted wreck, wreathed in steam and dripping water on the cobblestones outside the front door. It cost him £175. Father, horrified at first sight, showed some pride as year by year the engine was restored to the magnificence of its pristine days.

Repair work in progress. Restoration took 14 years.

Not every woman has had a steamroller named after her.

Drunken cronies banished, children installed in the tender.

High wind in the High Peak. A hitch on the road to Chatsworth. No casualties.

'A pint or two helps to kill the pain.'

Living van housed family, food and coal.

Going down. Descent by bosun's chair from top of church tower.

'Nice and peaceful up there with the birds.'

Scaffolding round chimney top – 'a work of art.'

Fly on the wall. Buzzing far afield. Fred tackles a restoration job on the old destructor chimney at Cambridge.

Educational visit to the back yard workshop.

After-dinner speaking. In-flight refuelling.

'A shock to discover how far my notoriety's spread.'

Traction engine. Taking shape after 12 year's work.

Resplendent new bedroom, sole occupant.

Toppled chimney. Nobody killed, nothing damaged. A good day.

Building the pyre at the chimney base.

Starting the fire that will bring the chimney down.

Steeplejack and new bride.

The renowned giant tractor Atlas in for a repair job.

Lighter work. A line in weathercocks.

Atlas, mended for delivery.

Old roller in a modern landscape.

LEGALIZED VANDALISM

ONE SPRING Fred got the job of demolishing the last decorative chimney top in Bolton. It was at the magnificent multi-storey Swan Lane mill, and it was a tight job. The bricks and the ornamental coping stones could not be dropped down the chimney because it was still in use to carry away the fumes of an oil boiler working at the bottom. They could not be thrown down the outside because the only open space between buildings was a narrow yard where people and vehicles passed. So Fred rigged up his flying buckets – two counterbalanced tubs on an endless rope running between Fred on his scaffolding 220 feet up and Donald Paiton down in the yard. Fred filled his bucket with a hundredweight of bricks and broken stone, released a brake and down it sailed. Donald emptied the contents on to a growing stack and the bucket soared up to the scaffolding, passing the other loaded bucket on its way down. They had 40 feet of chimney top to take off weighing about 50 tons:

'I invented this contraption in my head during the two years of enforced idleness while I was doing my National Service. I used to see the old steeplejacks in the forties and fifties tackling similar jobs. Those lads had it hard. They'd very little tackle and nobody exerted much mental effort to make it easier for them. It took ten of them to do the job. They'd commandeer a skip from the mill and fasten ropes to each corner. Then from up the chimney they'd haul the skip up, fill it with as many bricks as they thought suitable and cautiously lower it down. They had a tail rope going over a

97

block at the top and down to the men below who tied the end round a lamp post.

'It was a slow job. The skip came down at about two miles an hour and then it would only have about 56 lbs of brick in it. The job took months.

'One day, lying smoking on my army bed, it dawned on me that if you had a brake drum on the haulage system you could let it work by gravity and control it mechanically, single-handed. So when I was demobbed I went to the scrapyard and got a brake drum off a 1947 Rover motorcar. I'd no clear idea what I was aiming at. I tried all sorts of variations until I ended up with the contraption that's working here. It's a bit like driving a tram. The brake's like a dead man's handle. It's on all the time. When the bucket's full I just lift the lever. Down it goes, the empty one comes back up, and the brake goes on again. It runs so smoothly with such little wear that I'm still using the rope I bought fifteen years ago. God knows what the factory inspector would think about that.

'In taking this 40 feet off the top of the chimney the beginning is the most dangerous part of the job. The fancy top is made up of coping stones 2 feet long by 14 inches broad and about 8 inches thick. The brickwork on the inside of the chimney acts as a counterbalancing weight to the stones and it's rotten. In some places you can see daylight straight through the chimney stack. If I'm not careful when I disturb it the whole lot could collapse and shatter my scaffolding to matchwood.

'The stone blocks are too big to go into the bucket so I have to smash them with the sledgehammer. Some of the bigger pieces I load up weigh 60 to 80 pounds. I wouldn't risk shifting anything heavier. You've got to bear in mind that, even if you have the strength to lift them and the balance to carry them, the combined weight of yourself and the rock might be enough to go through the plank you're walking on.

'At the loading point the scaffolding is two planks thick. You'd need a fair amount of weight to snap that in two.

'The job is to get this 40 feet off without killing myself, or anybody else, or letting any bricks fly off to the detriment of somebody's windows or motorcar. You always have trouble from cars. We tied up a big heavy rope down below to keep them out of the danger area but they just untied it and carried on regardless. In the old days people would have treated our rope with some respect. They'd have thought: "It must be here for a purpose, we won't go through there." But not now. Parking the car is the priority even at the risk of death.

'When these chimneys were built things went slower. Only horses and carts went past and everybody knew if there was somebody mending the chimney up above. Now they know nothing. They zoom in from nowhere in their motorcar, jump out and leave it. Then if I lift a brick and a bit of mortar blows off – ping, there's a dent in the car roof and that's eighty quid up my shirt.

We can work at this job in fairly rough windy weather but not in rain. It turns the old mortar on the bricks into liquid grinding paste that wears your fingers away. If you keep picking up the bricks and throwing them into the buckets you end up at teatime with your finger ends bleeding. You can't wear gloves because they make your handling clumsy and dangerous. It's too easy to let one slip. In the dry the bricks are not nearly so abrasive. Your fingers last for weeks. They recover every night when you go to bed.

'What I wouldn't attempt in the wind is to shift the scaffolding. If you're foolish enough to try that you can do quite a lot of damage. The plank gets entangled in the rope and it'll go neither up nor down. It flies about like a kite in the gale.

'The job is a bit upsetting to me because this is the last chimney in Bolton with an ornamental top. When I've finished there'll be nothing left in town but cylindrical piles of bricks.

'All this beautiful fancy work that I'm destroying is not really in too bad a state. I could put it right. I'd dearly like to mend it and make it glorious again. With the holes repaired and the chimney stack pointed and fortified with iron bands it would be right for a hundred years. But it's redundant. Nobody loves it. They've no use for it any more. There's no black smoke coming up to be propelled high into the atmosphere. All they have below now is a little toy oil boiler.

'When I look at these beautiful terracotta blocks I'm smashing up I sometimes discover inside the fingermarks of the bloke who made them. I've saved one complete ring of these fancy stones and out of them I'm going to make the edging of a flower bed in my garden.

What we're doing is legalized vandalism. We're wrecking things of beauty that can never be replaced. When I went to art school, as I mentioned earlier, I was always drawing spinning mills and canals and pithead gear. People shook their head. "Dark satanic mills," they'd say.

'But they have a strange sort of beauty that Lowry captured in his paintings. There was marvellous architecture in those arched windows, the spotless engine houses with their giant flywheels and the big tall chimneys with fancy tops. There was never a more impressive sight than a spinning mill of several storeys working at night with the lights on, shining through all the windows.

'Swan Lane mill here was like a Greek palace with gold leaf decoration and fancy cast-iron. Some mills that have survived have been shotblasted and you can see what they were like when they were first built and stood in fields. They're magnificent, beyond comparison with anything that's been put up in the last fifty years.

'And what takes their place when they're knocked down? Estates of ticky-tacky houses that look from above like a collection of egg boxes. Or industrial estates, as they're pretentiously styled, industrial complexes. What they amount to is a big flat windswept area with a maze of roads serving a collection of tin, asbestos and plastic sheds. They've hardly any windows and more often than not an unpronounceable sign on the side. They don't call them Joe Brown Boilermaker any more. It's some fancy name that means nothing.

'No chimneys, no engines, nothing impressive and great. They're all plugged in with their Black and Deckers. The great age of technology! I've more machinery in my backyard than some of these firms. In fact many of them are making nothing. They just assemble or package other people's imported goods. We've become a nation of con men, making a living by selling each other double glazing. Everybody's trying to rip everybody else off. People all seem to be out for what they can get as quick as they can get it, as though there's some mad race before we all get blown up. Napoleon was prophetic, even if he wasn't right at the time – we are a nation of shopkeepers.

'In the old days, when Britain was great, people manufactured things and they worked hard at it for a long time every day, from seven in the morning, it might be, till half past five at night.

'Manual work has become a thing of the past. When you look at the state of this country, or what's left of it, there are loads of manual jobs that need doing. But they remain undone and millions of people stay out of work.

'When the civil war in America cut off cotton supplies in the last century they took the cotton spinners here out of the mills and had them digging reservoirs to give them something to do and keep them off the breadline. Those reservoirs are valuable. We're still using them. Can you imagine anything like that happening now?

'In the heyday of Swan Lane mill they had, I believe, ten big Lancashire boilers, all in a row, guzzling up hundreds of tons of coal every week. The other day I found an engineer's stock book in a waste bin. At one time they had 1,900 tons of coal in stock. From 1942 until some time in the late fifties they'd never less than 900 tons in the yard. Then all of a sudden it's down to 17 tons. You can guess what had happened. The next entry isn't in tons but in gallons, 18,000 gallons – of oil.

'The boilers had gone. The black smoke, which had been for 150 years the ceiling of our world, was disappearing from the sky. In the old days it used to rise all day in great rolling clouds from a forest of mill chimneys. Then at half past five when people came home from work the house fires started and smoke began to pour from the chimney pots of the rows and rows of terraced houses. We saw the sun for only a few days in the year and then as a pasty light. Everything was covered in soot. When you brushed against a privet hedge you'd blacken your shirt. When you blew your nose your hankie was black. It had a lovely acrid smell, of carbon and sulphur. It killed people before their time, of course. Now it's gone, banished by the Clean Air Act.

'The wealth of Britain, when it was wealthy, was founded on coal. I can remember when the whole town throbbed to those beautiful great steam engines that drove the mill machinery. The engineer would clean them down on Saturday mornings so they looked like exhibits in a science museum and when he had done no living soul, including the manager and the mill owner himself, would be allowed to set foot on the polished engine room floor.

When I first started climbing chimneys there were still quite a lot of places on coal and I even had the great pleasure of working at one or two where they still shovelled it on by hand.

'The black smoke rotted all the gutters in the neighbourhood and all the old dears' lace curtains, but working on the chimney tops you could avoid it. You could sit there all day pointing the brickwork or painting iron bands and it would sail past the end of your nose. You could get up and actually walk round the scaffolding through the stuff and come out the other side feeling not too bad.

'But coal has gone and industry everywhere, or what's left of it, has gone over to oil. It was an error in the first place to develop the petrol engine when everybody could have been happily and sedately propelled by steam. But it is a calamity to have turned industry over to oil, vulnerable to wars, OPEC, civil commotion, international finance and, most of all, exhaustion when in Britain alone we have three thousand years' reserve of coal ready to be dug up at our leisure.

'These little oil-burning boilers they use now don't need proper chimneys to carry their fumes up into the atmosphere. New chimneys these days are nothing more than glorified tin whistles. What comes from oil burning isn't proper smoke. It's a warm dampish sort of blue haze that makes you cough and splutter worse than Capstan full strength. Coal smoke billowing up the inside made a chimney nice and warm to work on. This stuff, feebly curling up, takes half an hour to reach the top and there's no heat left in it.

'The change might have been good for the health of the nation but it hasn't been good for mine. Often you can't escape oil smoke because it's not visible and, because there are no convection currents to shoot it into the atmosphere, it doesn't get away. It hangs round the top of the chimney and curls down the side. If a gale's blowing you're all right and even with a steady moderate wind you know which way it's going, but in calmer conditions you can find yourself working in it without noticing it. I can tell when that's happened. I'm not very hungry when I get home and I wake up next morning with my eyes stuck together and my throat sore not wanting to go anywhere near a chimney. I think it's twice as poisonous as coal smoke. It'll rot your chisel away if you leave it on a chimney top for a fortnight. It's like having your mouth round somebody's exhaust pipe. God knows what the state of my lungs must be with the number of cigarettes I smoke and having that lot as a double bonus.

'My mother and Alison are always warning me about smoking so much and I know that's good advice.

'I've also been criticized for letting it be known that I sometimes have a few pints at lunchtime before climbing back up the chimney. I'd like to say that my critics should come and try this job sober. When you're bashing away with a big hammer for hours on end a pint or two helps. it kills some of the pain.

'You wouldn't want to overdo it. You don't want to come out of the pub walking sideways. That could be very dangerous, peering over the scaffolding with half a hundredweight of rock in your arms.

'When I've had a couple of pints, I take it that little bit easier and more cautiously. I don't think I'm King Kong. Once you've got as far as the top of the first ladder coming up, one false move and you're dead.

'There are a million things that can go wrong. The scaffolding looks solid enough from below but it's uneven where the ropes are tied at the corners and there are gaps between the boards. If you put your foot through you might not fall off but you could smash your leg in two places, and then who could come to the rescue? The fire brigade's no good because their ladder isn't long enough. Somebody would have to come in a helicopter. But then the rotors might blow me off. Anyway, it'd be bad for my image to have to be rescued by a helicopter.

'Some kind people, concerned for my welfare and comfort, have asked in relation to my lunchtime drinking how at the top of a chimney the calls of nature might be met.

'It's never been much of a problem. People don't notice me working up chimneys except when I do a climb for charity and crowds turn up hoping to see me fall off. If there's no boiler at the bottom you can let fly down the middle of the chimney or, if the brickwork's high enough for concealment, over the side, whereby the people below might gain the impression that it's raining in the next field.

'On one occasion I was working up a chimney with another steeplejack. We'd had a few pints and we made use of a bucket half full of cement water. At the end of the afternoon we emptied it over the side of the ship. The wind caught it and it splattered a magnificent new bright red Alpha Romeo sports car. When we got down the owner was staring in disbelief at these white urinated-cement spots drying lovely in the sun all over his beautiful car. We got a bucket of water and wiped it clean. We went away without enlightening him about what had rained on his car.

'At the end of the day the old steeplejacks used to tie their rope round the nearest lamp post and go home. Life's not as simple as that now. If we leave access to the ladders we get midnight climbers proving themselves, especially at weekends. We usually remove the bottom ladder.

'That didn't prevent one daring character from having a go. He came out of the pub, took his shoes and socks off and, like a monkey, scaled the stonework up to where the ladders began. At quarter to midnight he was shouting and screaming up in the darkness. He could get no further up and he couldn't get down. Fortunately he was stuck just within the range of a fire brigade turntable ladder. Somebody coaxed him down and they carted him off to the infirmary suffering from hyperthermia.

'I can't really criticize these lads because I did the same thing in my young days. They're not all wild men. Some of them have real talent and no outlet for it. A man came to watch a felling I did recently, chap on a motorbike, leather boots, leather jacket, hair halfway down his back, but there was something about him. He knew the names of all the steeplejacking firms for miles around.

'I remembered then having met him once before when he begged me to let him climb my chimney. I weighed him up. He was no fool. I invited him to come round the next day. He was a natural, straight up the ladders. He said he'd never been up before except once when he climbed up drunk in the dark. He took to it like a duck to water. That lad would have a shining future – if only there were more chimneys left.

'The people who really annoy me are the enterprising vandals who come in the night when we've left the rope unsecured and cut it in two with a piece of broken glass.

It could be an 800-foot coil of rope worth, £200. The only answer is to spend time before I go home tying the rope in to every other ladder and more time in the morning unlashing it. That way they can't get at it. Even if they're caught they're not taught any lesson. "Poor little lad," they say. "He's had a hard upbringing. He's nothing else to occupy his mind."

'The days of tying the rope to the lamp post and going away happy are past. Times have changed, and not for the better.'

IN THE PUBLIC EYE

THE FIRST documentary film in which Fred appeared, in 1979, caused something of a stir. It won a few awards and was shown by the BBC several times. On Fred, a lifelong loner, it inflicted instant fame. He found himself a minor celebrity.

It was a role in which he was never to be quite comfortable. It brought in some money, though not on a scale to supplant his regular job. He was surprised and perhaps a little flattered to be recognized by strangers. He had always liked to talk and amuse people and his notoriety, as he came to call it, gave him a ready audience whenever he felt moved to hold forth. But the huge celebrity industry is very much a product of what Fred condemns as 'the modern world' – the non-events and the bogus personalities, the desperate striving for recognition, the frantic salesmanship of nothing, the groundlings' gawping reverence of publicized nonentities, the screaming mass adulation of slight talent.

Nothing could have been more at odds with Fred's Victorian values and forthright behaviour. He approached his bit of fame warily and in some bewilderment, as he explained:

'This celebrity business is all right if only you could escape from it when you wished. It's hampered my progress on my steam engines. At one time I could go into my backyard shed after tea and work undisturbed until 3.00 a.m. if I wanted to. Nobody mithered me. Now the phone's going all the time, life insurance men, double glazing salesmen, people wanting me to be present at some event or just to have a talk. I can spend half the night traipsing between the shed and the house.'

'Sometimes characters I don't know come strolling down to the shed and park themselves there for the evening. I don't mind talking to anybody who has a genuine interest in steam, but often I'd just like to sit alone in my shed and be quiet or go into a pub with people I know and listen to what they've got to say – though you've got to put a word in sometimes or they'd think you were propped up dead in the corner.

'It's not unusual for people motoring about on holiday to make a diversion and come knocking on the door, all poised to inspect me and my premises, but without any kind of serious interest in what I do. I've learned to weigh these tourists up and to let in only those who seem capable of asking intelligent questions.

'Foreigners come. A gang of Americans, some of them wearing sombreros, pitched up and set fire to my parlour. They said they were steeplejacks and they were making a video on English churches. They wanted me to say a few words on the subject. It seems that their equipment runs at a different voltage from ours but they said their rectifying equipment would cope with that. So they plugged their lights in and I got out all the photograph albums of jobs that I've done and the interview was going quite well when suddenly there's a blinding flash and a bloody great explosion, the lights go out, the carpet's on fire, the flames are licking at the furniture.

'By the time we'd beaten everything out our American friends were on their way to France or wherever they were marauding next.

'Some good things come out of the publicity. After the first film was shown on BBC television we had nice letters from all over England, some with generous offers. A bloke in Birmingham rang up and said, I've got just the thing here for you. It's a hand-operated steam valve reseating machine. I'm fed up of falling over it. If you'll come and collect it, you can have it."

'A firm of manufacturers wrote: "Dear Mr Dibnah, We were

deeply disturbed to see that your matches keep blowing out when you are on the top of chimneys, so we enclose herewith a sample of our windproof and waterproof matches."

'They were like welding rods. They stayed red and glowing for a couple of minutes after the flame went out.

'One Sunday morning a lady of ninety was delivered round by her son. Her husband who'd died had been a steam enthusiast and, according to the son, seeing our film made her happy again. Apparently it was the first time she'd smiled since her husband passed on.

'Suddenly, it seemed, everybody wanted to know about steeplejacks. I'd been climbing up chimneys for more than twenty years and nobody took a grain of notice. When I've finished a job for a company nobody's ever had enough interest to climb up and see what I've done. Now crowds turn up to watch me climb at charity events, and even on ordinary working days a bit of an audience can gather at the chimney bottom.

'When I was a boy I don't think anybody but me watched steeplejacks. We were so busy as a nation then that on weekdays nobody could afford to stand about watching a man put red ladders up a chimney and at weekends they were too knackered to be interested. I suppose people now come to my climbs for charity because once they've mowed the lawn they're bored with sitting at home and they turn out in anticipation of seeing somebody come to a nasty end.

'Once I was standing on a platform at Birmingham station and an Indian bloke I'd never seen before came up and said, "Are you the man who climbs chimneys?"

'It's a shock to discover how widely my notoriety has spread. Another time we were driving down the motorway going to Gloucester in the Landrover which has my name painted on the door, and a motorcoach overtook us with all the passengers on the near side waving through the windows. Then the coach slowed down and, as we went past, all the people on the other side had a wave.

'It makes you feel very conspicuous, and sometimes the pressure gets at you. In pubs people look at you, they don't speak, they just keep staring. It makes you very self-conscious and uncomfortable. Then some who are a bit braver approach and say, as one actually did recently, "I hope you don't mind me calling you Fred."

'God forbid. Who do they think I am? I'm not a pop star or an actor or a television front person. I'm just a bum who climbs chimneys.

'The pressure builds up, it gets to you. Even at steam engine rallies, where I'd been known and gone unnoticed for years, people with cameras are after me now. "Stand there. Do that. Pose with Jack and Mabel." I must have had my photo taken with a dozen babies at the last steam weekend. You take to sneaking off and hiding where nobody can find you. But even in the act of slipping away, nipping along as inconspicuously as you can, you can be nabbed, stopped and photographed. It gets hard going after a couple of days.

'Long before my notoriety spread I was in the habit of taking my steamroller to local charity events for Dr Barnardos and other good causes. Some of them rewarded me with enough bags of coal to get to the next do, and so it went on nice and gently through the summer.

'With the non-charity events I'm asked to now, I've learned to pick and choose. Some such as garden parties, fetes and agricultural shows might well be agreeable, but I could only take them on at a loss. Somebody will ring up and offer me £25 and, often as an afterthought, ask me to bring the engine. They seem to think it's like a motorcar – you just open the garage door, turn a key and chuff, chuff, chuff up the garden path.

'It's not like that. You need the best part of a day to get it ready, polishing and cleaning. You've got to light the fire and get up steam, then at four to five miles an hour travelling is going to take half a day. You need 5 cwt of coal and quite an amount of oil – the oil doesn't go round for ever, it's a dead loss system whereby most of it finishes on your face and your shirt. It could easily cost more than the fee, quite apart from taking up a lot of time.

'After dinner speaking is the one new line of business that has developed through the publicity, and there again I've learned with experience what to take on and what to say "No thanks" to.

'I go down best with engineering societies, planning departments of town halls, people of that sort who are interested in my subjects. It's no use going to a rugby club because they're all great lads, but all they want is quickfire jokes so they can down six pints and go on talking among themselves at the same time.

'At lots of places it's an uphill task. Round Table men are a bit on the wild side when they've had too much lemonade. I reckon at eighty per cent of their dinners I've mastered them. I've never had any flak like shouting and answering back, but in some audiences I've encountered a total lack of interest which I've not been able to overcome.

'Many people who go to these dinners feel they've had a speaker forced upon them they would never have chosen, and when it gets late, businessmen in particular are resistant to being entertained. They've all been at work that day, and I'm told – though I find it hard to believe – that working with your brain is just as tiring as working with your hands. If the early part of the programme drags on too long, if the chairman can't resist the temptation to saw on, you find yourself, at some time after ten o'clock, with an audience that's very tired and very drunk. Thankfully there is always somebody in the audience who's interested, and all you can do is to talk to him and pretend the rest of them aren't there. I've heard of speakers in this situation who have stood up and said: "Well gentlemen, I have a speech in my pocket which would have lasted an hour and a half but, as you are like you are, I shall sit down again and that's it. Good night."

'I don't think I could bring myself to do that. Most places are well organized with a responsive audience and I've had some very enjoyable evenings on these engagements.

'Time, again, limits the number of speaking engagements I can take on. Travelling, as I do, by Landrover or by train I can't range far without making too great inroads on my working time.

'In my kind of job getting ready is not just a question of scrubbing my teeth and brushing down the remaining strands. It's the full scouring and scrubbing treatment. By the time I'm presentable the early part of the evening has gone. I've learned not to knock off work early and I'm cautious about accepting daytime engagements, opening offices and things. Once the drinks cabinet is opened, the imbibing inevitably seems to go on to midnight and the earlier I start the more I'm inclined to drink.

'It can affect the job badly. If you're losing half a day twice a week and going to work next morning with a hangover, a long tedious job like chucking bricks down from the top of a chimney becomes interminable. It's like going to the same spot every day from the dawn of Creation. Every hammer blow rings through your head and you suffer. I've worked often enough with a hangover to know I've just got to bear it and work my way through it. I always say I'll never do it again, but when I get talking the pints keep arriving and the top of the chimney tomorrow morning seems a long way off. Getting too much pop down is my downfall.

'One thing that does annoy me, people will sail up and say, "You must have made a fortune out of it."

'Then when I deny that I've made a fortune some man of vision arrives on the doorstep and suggests I should have. If I'll place myself in his hands he'll manage my affairs as agent for a percentage, sometimes specified, usually not.

'At first I'd no idea what kind of fee was usual for public events. I got twenty quid here and forty quid there. At one

Rotarian do I was given two sacks full of rivets for my new boiler – which were very welcome. I now get about £250 for an after-dinner speech, which I believe is the going rate.

'One of the best money-raising things was a television commercial I made early on for a local brewery. I never realized it took such a huge crew to make a short advert for beer. We did about 999 takes of every scene which kept us in the pub all day long. We had to have a taxi home afterwards. We'd all had too much pop.

'Television commercials are the big earners, but I've only been asked to do three over ten years. I get tired of people speculating about the astronomical amounts I'm supposed to have made. You never know who's listening and it may include the tax man. In fact I can state what there is to show for all these endeavours. I bought a house as a sitting tenant for £5,000 in cash. I bought an old wreck of a steam tractor for £2,300 and I had some jobs done on it at engineering works which I might not otherwise have been able to afford. I extended my steam workshop, mainly from scrap, and I built the house extension, mainly with bricks from a demolition site. I also sustained the cost of a divorce. But that's the sum of it, unless you count another second-hand army Landrover to replace the one that was surplus from the Second World War. I don't complain about that. What's the sense, even if you've got the money, of putting it into a motorcar that will only rust away when you can travel on a steam engine which steadily increases in value as the years go by?

'Again, some people say my business must have benefited, and it's certainly true that in recent years I've been contracted for well-paid jobs in other parts of the country to topple chimneys whose proprietors might have been inspired with confidence by jobs that went right on the television screen. That's one good thing about film. If you do it night in front of the camera, it's right every time it's shown. If you do it wrong, nobody will ever know because the camera crew will be buried in the rubble.

'We got one outrageous invitation on the 'phone to work in exotic climes. "This is the Such-and-Such Sugar Corporation. We have two chimney in Barbados. We'd like you to come and knock the top fifty feet off." We didn't take them up. Donald didn't like the idea of camping out so he wouldn't go, and I didn't think I'd look very good up the ladder with my knobbly knees sticking out of Bermuda shorts.

'But mine isn't a business than can increase much, however many inquiries we get. I'm limited to the amount of work I can do by the length of a working day which is limited in winter by the hours of daylight and at any time by human endurance. My business is a one-man band, two counting my assistant. just occasionally we take on casual help. I've never wanted to expand it beyond that. It would restrict my freedom. If I want to stay at home and play with my steam engines I can do. I don't have employees standing round the back door waiting for orders. I don't want more paperwork than I have already and I don't want to be troubled with all the safety regulations that would apply if I had regular employees.

'Summing up the benefits of my bit of fame, I haven't made a fortune but I've made enough to enjoy life without the financial worry we had at one time when we didn't know where the next hundred quid was coming from and the tax man was banging on the door. I'm glad it happened. I've more freedom and a lot more variety. I enjoy seeing new places and meeting different kinds of people. I'm more relaxed than I've ever been. I face the approach of old age without anxiety.

'Some people have strange ideas about promoting their products. The 'phone went and somebody said, "Will you come to Old Trafford and run over a computer with your steam engine?" They made a worthwhile offer, so I got up steam and went.

'On a forecourt outside the bar, they'd built with large polystyrene panels the walls of what was supposed to be an office, pleasingly occupied by a young lady sitting at a computer keyboard. About a hundred guests holding their drinks were ushered out and lined up along the bar side of the "office". I was stationed with the roller out of sight on the forecourt. At a signal I chuffed up and broke through the "office" wall. Everybody was surprised, some were amused, all contrived to laugh. End of story. I quite enjoyed doing the steam part of the job, I got well paid for it, and if it fits in with what these modern people want, I suppose everybody's pleased.

'I've noticed in doing these promotional things for big companies how many good jobs there are and I've sometimes felt a bit envious of the lifestyle that goes with them. But then I think perhaps the job is a bind to them, and I suppose you'd soon get fed up of going to a swanky pub for lunch every day when you could be sitting on top of a chimney and surveying the town with a flask of coffee and a newspaper full of chips.

'I've learned to pick my public appearance jobs. I've been asked to do stupid things that I feel embarrassed about. People have said that I've looked out of place and they're right. Events like a glamorous grandmother competition. What the hell do I know about glamorous grandmothers?

'I did the cat show, though. I enjoyed that, mainly because I had a good cat-up-a-chimney story to tell. I must admit at the outset that I'm not really a cat man. We've had four in our time and three have come to grief. First one, somebody shot it. The next one got poisoned and just faded away and the one after that went bad. The wife took it to the vet, spent fifteen quid on pills for it, brought it back and it was dead ten minutes later. So I told her to take the pills back and get a rebate – which she did. The story I told at the cat show was more suitable for the audience of thousands of cats and their owners.

'I arrived one winter morning at the bottom of a 160-foot chimney and found a ginger tom cat perched part way up the bottom ladder. I climbed nice and slowly to avoid alarming it but before I was in grabbing range it shot up to the next ladder above. What I should have done was to have run fast up the ladder. There's no way it could have climbed quick enough to prevent me overtaking it. But I didn't want to scare it.

'I went to see the mill manager and asked him to ring the fire brigade to come with their turntable ladder. They're a bit tight, these mill men. "No," he said, "if we ring up the fire brigade they'll send a bill. We'll ring the RSPCA. They have an arrangement with the fire brigade, so we'll get the job done for nowt."

'We had a cup of tea and a talk about steam engines, by which time the RSPCA man had gone to work with such effect that the cat was now 130 feet up the chimney. He'd brought a piece of conduit piping with a string threaded through it, with which he hoped to lasso the cat. How he'd have managed to throw it I don't know. He didn't have the chance. As he went up, the cat went further up. He came back down flummoxed.

'So then it was my turn. The cat moved off the ladder and out on to a ledge. I climbed quietly past it to the top of the chimney. The brickwork there was encrusted with about half a ton of soot, deposited through the years. I threw a handful of it down, meaning to urge the cat back to the ladder and down.

'It had the opposite effect. It must have thought, "There's life up there. I'll keep on going." So it went back to the ladder and up. Six feet short of the top it moved out on to another ledge three inches wide, where I couldn't reach it and didn't dare to try to disturb it. I went back to the bottom, by then so blackened by the smoke from the chimney that I looked like Al Jolson. By now the RSPCA man had got a beautiful big plastic basket. We tied four pieces of rope to the corners and put in a tempting bait of cat meat. Up I went to the top again and dangled the basket within range of the cat. The cat moved round on its ledge. I moved round with it on the chimney top. We must have gone round two dozen times. I don't think cats really like me. It just wouldn't get into the basket.

'We took a break for lunch and went through the same sort of performance in the afternoon until darkness approached. In the meantime the event had been on lunchtime television and 'phone calls started arriving at our house. One person had told Alison, "What you want is a goldfish bowl with a mouse in it. You dangle the bowl down attached to strings and the cat'll jump in after the mouse."

'Some other bright spark suggested we should get a plastic drainpipe 160 feet long, knock the cat into it at the top and catch it in a coal bag at the bottom.

'The RSPCA man kept his spirits up by saying as darkness fell that in the cold of the night the cat would be hungry and come down of its own accord. I thought at the time that it might be wishful thinking.

'It rained all night. Next morning the cat was still up on its ledge, no longer ginger but a bedraggled dirty black. I went up to assess the situation again and decided to put up a staging round the chimney just below the ledge. I could then knock the cat off the ledge with reasonable certainty that it would land on the plank.

'When I got back to the ground a man came out of the crowd and said, "We've a volunteer here from Animals in Distress. He's very good at catching cats in high places."

'"We don't want no bloody heroes," the manager said. "Get him out of the place."

'So that was the end of him, as we thought.

'We went away to organize the equipment. When we arrived back a police van and an ambulance were standing in the yard and the volunteer was at the top of the chimney. He'd got the cat – he must have had a talent for that – but he was stuck. He had the cat in one hand and with the other he clung to the ladder. He couldn't move.

'When I got up to him he was in a bad state, poor fellow. Smoke from a mill chimney won't kill you but it doesn't half make your nose run. He had two candles running out of his nose, round the side of his mouth and dripping from his chin. But he held resolutely on to the cat.

'I told him how to move his legs so he could free both his hands for holding the cat. He did well and we made some distance down. Then I thought of a better plan. I got the cat box pulled up on a rope, held it close to the volunteer and snapped the lid down when he placed the cat in it.

'We lowered the box down, then I descended with the volunteer. He was a brave tenacious man. The police arrested him. I never saw him again.'

TRACTION ENGINE

'By 1980 my steamroller was just about completely restored. It was practically brand new again. The boiler was new, the tank, the axles, the gears, the funnel, the piston rods – everything except the castings.

'It will be my memorial. But, as I've said, steamrollers do have some inherent shortcomings as a means of transport. What I'd always really wanted was a traction engine with springs and rubber tyres and two wheels on the front instead of the 2-ton dead weight of the roller. It wouldn't knock your teeth out or make you bite the end of your tongue when you went over a manhole cover. It would romp along painlessly at sixteen miles an hour.

'There's a lot of competition for buying traction engines that have been done up, or there was until the recession, and many people have been taken in by appearances. They can be done up to look beautiful, but when they move they sound like a steel band gone wild. They're a paintjob with the paint covering a multitude of mechanical sins. There's more of those about than good ones. But I couldn't have afforded one that had been done up in any way, well or badly. What I was looking for was a rusty wreck that nobody would compete for, a tractor in the state of the roller when I first bought it. I was confident that, however bad it was, I would be capable of doing the job. In fourteen years of work on the roller I'd served my apprenticeship. I'd got together a grand collection of tools and I'd discovered engineering works that would do a good job cheap.

'I felt differently about it at different times. Some days when I'd been at the pop and didn't feel too well it looked like another sentence to hard labour. Other days I thought, "I'm still young enough to be confident of seeing one more big job through. If I don't buy one now I might regret it for the rest of my days."

'Alison had an enlightened attitude, particularly in view of the domestic upsets caused by the long haul of doing up the roller. She considered that travelling faster and more smoothly we'd be able to keep on going to steam rallies in our old age with less danger of popping off on the way. I think she also thought it would keep me out of the pub at nights and on Sundays. She'd have me in the backyard locked up in the shed.

'As a matter of fact I had, by then, tracked down an old Aveling tractor. It belonged to Peter Froud, now sadly departed, who had a number of steam vehicles and long boats. We'd met at a steam rally when our engines collided when we were both slightly under the influence.

'The main part of the engine was in a corner of his big hangar on the back of a lorry draped with cobwebs. People who didn't know wouldn't have recognized it as a traction engine or indeed any kind of vehicle. It looked just like a rusty box studded with rivets. The wheels and the crank and other odds and ends were propped against the wall. Peter produced what he called "a box of goodies" which turned out to be a collection of small parts. We agreed on £2,300.

'I think Alison had some misgivings when I brought the pieces home to the shed in the autumn of 1980. The last one had at least arrived home under its own steam. "It needs a lot done to it," she said. "How are we going to find money for everything that needs to be done?"

'"We managed before," I said. "No more holidays."

'"But we've never had any holidays," she protested.

'Which was something of an exaggeration. We had a holiday when we went to Gretna Green for our honeymoon. I assured her I could make the old wreck very beautiful and a pleasure to ride on.

'I reckoned to finish the job in four years, which was over-optimistic. I've done a lot of work on it, but twelve years have now passed and I've still a lot more to do on it before the paint goes on.

'There have been distractions. Life hasn't been as simple as it was in the fourteen-year period when I was working on the roller. There's the celebrity business, which bites into the time I can spend in my shed. Then there's been a lot of work on the house. Once I'd tackled the bulge in the back wall and got the tie rods through to prevent it collapsing into the river, Alison pressed me to start on the two-storey extension to give a bit more room to the growing family.

'Then, in order to do the traction engine job as it should be done, I decided to build a complete steam-driven workshop in my backyard so that practically all the jobs on the tractor and any future steam engines could be done on the premises. That meant hours of scouring scrapyards and months of engineering work. It left less time to work on the traction engine itself but I don't regret it. I need to be able to do everything possible myself. The more that engineering works are modernized the harder it is to find anybody outside for these old-fashioned jobs.

'An example is the trouble I had getting the casting made for the front end. I took the pattern to a locomotive works where after a month pondering on the matter they decided they couldn't do it. So I went to another foundry that had been modernized. It was nice and clean and beautiful, equipped with benches. Nobody was dirty. They just looked at the drawing and said, "Sorry, we can't do that for you, pal. Try up the road."

'The place they sent me to couldn't have been more different. It was just like 1890 again – an inch of muck over the walls and these old boys with flat caps crawling about in black sand all over the floor.

'"Aye, lad, we'll make it for you," the boss said. "Come and collect it tomorrow afternoon."

'It was beautiful, a perfect fit, straight on to the engine, no need for any grinding or fitting. Such places don't abound any more, which made me determined to handle as much as possible myself.

'Over the years I'd got together bit by bit a grand collection of old power tools which, as a temporary measure, I geared down the steamroller to drive. I rebuilt and extended the engine shed to house both engines and the machine tools, using second-hand materials. Because of the wholesale demolition that's been going on you can get cheap things like window frames that are practically new, having been put into a building perhaps only months before it was condemned. Railway sleepers made a good floor, so I've spared myself the old boys' daily practice of crawling about in the dirt. Later, I got a stationary engine to drive the machinery from a mill at Chadderton where I went to mend the chimney. I discovered it, rusty and neglected, in a cubby hole behind a door. It had first been installed to drive mechanical stokers on five Lancashire boilers when the mill was built in 1904. It needed a lot of work to make it look brand new again.

'The boiler I got is practically new – a Danks 3-throw 1964 model. I found it at a mill at Oswaldtwistle. There's no room for the boiler and the stationary engine by the engine shed, so they have a housing of their own, together with a three-foot circular saw, at the other end of the yard. The power is transmitted through a 120-foot iron shaft high above the ground – which we had quite a lot of fun getting installed. So my workshop saws up the wood that heats the boiler that drives the engine that turns the shaft that works the machinery that's going – some day – to finish the job on the traction engine.

'I do have my leg pulled about having made such slow progress. But there's no tearing hurry. The pleasure is in doing the job as near perfect as is humanly possible, never accepting second best because of feeling some pressure of time. I enjoy working on it in the shed. I also enjoy, within reason, knocking off and talking to people who call in.

'A traction engine is a thing of a more leisurely and painstaking age and the job should be enjoyed in a leisurely and painstaking way. I know from the last time that when the job is finally finished there's a sense of triumph and also of loss. The thing that's occupied your mind for years is done with. You've no more problems to brood over. You feel achievement and also a sense of anticlimax.

'There is only one fly in the ointment. One of my neighbours has taken a dislike to my steam engine activities and he's had the council round about pollution and smoke and noise.

'Steam itself isn't a pollutant. Whenever they mention pollution on the television they show pictures of the clouds of steam rising from power station cooling towers. There's no pollution in that. What they should show is chimneys emitting smoke.

'I can't see that my backyard workshop does any harm. One thing that tells me this is that the wildlife round here is flourishing. Squirrels have come to take up residence and last summer two woodpeckers nested in the tree nearest to the stationary engine shed. Now my boiler inspector is a birdwatcher and when I told him about them he came back after tea with his wife and a party of ornithologists to look at these woodpeckers through binoculars. So where's all the noise and aggro? It defies me.

'We came by a dog to guard all this valuable scrap iron. Nick, our little white mongrel, was an excellent animal, good about the house and keen on steam engine trips, but she got old and one Christmas the girls asked for another dog. We got a little terrier sort of thing. He looked like a mop without a stick. But one day he followed Donald out to the road and got run over. There was a terrible upset in the house. The kids were in tears. I got the shovel out and we gave him a respectful burial in the garden.

'The story got in the *Bolton Evening News* – Mr Dibnah's dog has just got flattened, the new pet dog for his kids. One of the readers rang us: "We've got a nice dog we'd like to give you with a pedigree and everything."

We expected a little one like we've always had. The man arrived on the doorstep with an Alsatian bitch. Alison was frightened to death of the thing but she got used to it. It was a nice dog, but it must have been kept in a backyard. It had no manners in the house and left dog hairs over everything. So I said, "It either goes back whence it came or it lives in a kennel in the yard as a guard dog."

'They all settled for that. So we had this wonderful dog guarding the workshop and the steam engines. She had a gruff bark. I made good progress with my jobs in the shed at night. Few mitherers came near while she was there.'

UPS AND DOWNS

THROUGH THE years the Dibnahs took their summer holidays in the form of weekend visits to steam rallies. One of the last they all went to was at Astle Park, Cheshire, in 1984, reached by two days' travelling.

Rain fell heavily throughout the second day. When they arrived the ground was sodden and the air grey and acrid from the smoke of the assembled engines. Water dripped everywhere and everybody was coughing.

In the living van Alison got out the things to start a meal. Fred traded tales with steam men under a canvas awning rigged up on the side of one of the engines. They were a loud rollicking lot. They filled the murk with laughter.

They remembered 'poor old Jim', one of their number recently departed who, although he was 74 and had a finger missing – lost in the flywheel – was revered for never, in his time, having stood for any 'messing about'.

'Do you remember those yobbos he flattened?' asked a big man in a boilersuit and a baseball cap. 'He was on the footplate of his engine and they were threatening to climb up and drive it. They thought he was an old man they could easily take on. "We're getting up," they said. "Advance no further," old Jim said. "Stop us," they challenged him and made a move.

'He said no more but got hold of his fire shovel and bang, bang, on the head of one and then the other. The ambulancemen came and carried them off.'

Gales of laughter. At the door of the living van Alison raised her voice to make herself heard. 'It's raining in, Fred. The beds are wet through.'

Fred stepped out from the awning. 'It can't be that bad. Put the bucket there until it stops dripping.'

'But there are two leaks; one over each bed.'

'Put the bowl under the other one.'

'I'm peeling the potatoes in the bowl.'

'What about that bucket there?'

'It's dirty.'

'Better dirty than wet.'

Fred passed up the dirty bucket. Alison went back in. Fred returned to the awning.

'Rain does have some benefits,' the man in the baseball cap said. 'It shows where your caravan roof leaks.'

'I know where it leaks, it's right over my bed.'

'Can't you tell the missis to sleep on the wet side?'

'No,' said Fred. 'She sleeps on her own on t' floor.'

The steam men rocked with laughter and coughed like far-gone consumptives in the haze of steam engine and cigarette smoke. Rain drummed on the tarpaulin.

For some time Alison had felt a yearning for bluer skies and gentler company beyond the range of their steamroller. Their last holiday, steam rallies apart, had been their honeymoon at Gretna Green. Now, with the eldest of their three daughters in her teens, Alison felt the time ripe for a second vacation.

It was not only that going to different steam rallies was variety enough for Fred, but also, it came to light, he still had a hang-up about holiday resorts caused by the desperate struggles in his childhood when he had fought like a cornered rat to avoid being loaded on to the day-trip bus for Blackpool. 'The damage' he ruefully explained, 'was done to me when I was quite small.'

Nevertheless he understood their wishes and one day, out of the blue, he promised to take them all to Blackpool for the better part of a week.

The sun shone. Fred, sitting on the sands unshaded by his cap, began to tan. He joined in. He tossed the beach ball to and fro with the girls. He took them riding on the donkeys. They went on the big dipper and the scenic railway. All he drew the line at was rolling up his trousers and paddling. Everybody was happy.

But after a couple of days the weather broke. Rain lashed the promenade. The sea broke in white-flecked grey rollers under a stormy sky. After breakfast, the Dibnahs, all five of them, hurried down the steps of the boarding house and piled into the cab of their old Landrover.

They drove along above the promenade. The beach was almost deserted. Four horse riders in the surf pressed on, heads down against the rain. A couple of brave landladies exercised their Alsatians. Holidaymakers, turned out of their lodgings, cowered in the promenade shelters.

Fred took a left turn inland, through the town and out to an industrial estate. He stopped outside a small engineering works. 'That's it. Let's get the ladders off.'

Above them rose a small brick chimney. 'That's the one we're knocking down.'

The holiday, it transpired, had come out of a deal Fred had made with the proprietor.

'One day I got a 'phone call from this chap who said, "I've got this chimney I want you to knock down at Blackpool."

'I said sorry, it was too far from home. He rang again and it came out in his rather persistent conversation that he was the proprietor of a boiler works, a sort of pressure vessel company. just the man we needed! I was short of a new front plate for the boiler of the traction engine. I popped over one weekend and showed him the drawing of what was wanted. He agreed to make it for me if I'd knock his chimney down. That's how we ended up here on our holidays.'

The rain was too heavy for the children to get out of the Landrover. They watched from the cab as Alison, anorak hood tied round her face, splashed along the puddled path, carrying ladders to the foot of the chimney.

Fred hammered the iron hooks into the chimney wall. Quickly and expertly the ladders were swung up and secured. Lightning flashed. Thunder rolled. Fred, now above the roof line, was hit by the full force of the gale.

'Come on, love,' he urged. 'Pull on this rope. I'm getting wet.'

'Alison seized on the idea of coming to Blackpool,' he said. 'I don't suppose she bargained for this kind of holiday, pulling ladders up a chimney in the pouring rain. She's pretty good at it, though she still has a bit of trouble tying the knots. One day some years ago she helped me to unladder a 200-footer. You learn to take the rough with the smooth in this job and today's bloody rough. That's the price she has to pay for coming to Blackpool on holiday.'

Next day the weather was better. Alison and the children went to the beach. Fred began work on the demolition of the chimney. It was an easy job, squatting astride the lightly built chimney wall, dislodging the bricks with a tap of the hammer and flinging them down. Seabirds swooped around. The bricks drummed into the skip below.

'It's a piece of cake, they come off so easy. It's just a matter of not dropping them through the roof on the men and machines working below. I'm happy doing this. It keeps me off the sands, sitting all day watching the tide go in and out and getting sunburned.'

Down in the works they had finished the front plate.

'What happened to your last one?' the workman asked.

'Gone rusty. Seventy years of the rain running down the funnel on to it.'

'Seventy years – you've had your whack out of it then.'

'Somebody has,' Fred said. 'Not me.'

He was delighted with the job and with the deal. 'Alison's a bit subdued about the laddering day when we all got soaked through, but it's worked out well. They're down on the beach building sandcastles and spending my money and I'm happy at getting summat for nowt, as you might say, quite a few bobs' worth of engineering for just knocking a little chimney down.

'They must be having a good time because at night they're all flaked out. You tuck 'em in bed and, whuff, they're off – they've gone – unconscious. It's turned out very nice for all of us.'

Fred's rosy view was not generally shared in the household. Alison persisted in requesting a proper holiday.

'I ask him every year. I say, "I would like a holiday, Fred. Other wives go on holiday. Why can't I?"'

What Alison meant was not Blackpool again, with or without ladders, but Greece, or some such place with blue skies and golden beaches abroad. That was the sticking point. Fred had been abroad once, when he was in the army, and he didn't like it. He said:

'There's nothing in Greece for a man like me, I shouldn't think. I believe there are some decent buildings to look at, but I just couldn't bear to lie there in the sand all day watching the sun shine. It isn't really my style.

'They're a bit vain, people who like that, aren't they? They lie there in the sun so when they come back to grotty old England everybody'll think, "Where on earth have they been? They must have been abroad." It's oneupmanship, isn't it, the holiday job?'

Fred dug in. Alison pressed on: 'The girls and I are going to Greece. He won't come with us, so we'll go alone. I've been married seventeen years and never been on a holiday abroad. We're going to enjoy ourselves and get sunburned. Fred, of course will be going to Stockport for an engine rally. He'll enjoy that and I'll enjoy my holiday.

'He is grown up now. I should imagine he'll manage all right. I'll wave him off for his weekend with the engine and I'll leave food for when he comes back in the freezer my mother gave us. He says he can cook eggs and chips and he'll be all right for tea and coffee so long as he doesn't forget and let the kettle boil dry, as he once did. It filled the house with a blue haze.

'I told him I'd booked the holiday. When he started complaining I went and paid for it so there was nothing he could do to stop it. He's very upset. In fact it's making him ill. But I'm still going on holiday.'

When he returned from his steam engine weekend Fred had his first taste of living alone. He saw the other side:

'The wife has never had a holiday, so she deserves a bit of summat, doesn't she, for seventeen years of putting up with me? I find it very quiet. I'm lonely. I can't settle to anything. I don't really know how to pass the time after work. I sit on the step outside listening to the birds singing. But I suppose it's quieter than having the kids playing records and there's nobody shouting at me, telling me what to do.

'I'm managing. I'm very good at cooking chips and frying eggs. That's one thing I learned in the army. I've only needed to wash up once.'

Many months of washing up lay ahead. It was in that first week that Fred, rather against his sense of propriety, painted the ironwork on the parish church clock gloss yellow for want of gold leaf. It was a dismal sign of the times which in Fred's immediate vicinity were changing fast.

'On their arrival back from Greece they informed me they wanted a divorce. They didn't like the world of steam engines and factory chimneys. I don't know why, because the chimneys have kept us all. Life was getting to a stage where we could look forward to being semi-retired. Now it looks like I'll have to raise money through a mortgage and work for another seventeen years to buy Alison a house and fix her up in the style she's become accustomed to.

'It's not so long ago that we were voted the happiest married couple in our steam engine club. But perhaps it's better this way. Alison wants the modern life and there's no way I'm going to change from being the Victorian tyrant I'm supposed to be. Discos and that sort of thing, those bloody coloured lights and all that banging – the whole shindig reminds me of the end of the Roman empire. Half of them have gone queer – there's pubs now for queers – and the other half have minds that are working all the time towards pleasure. Everything has to be pleasure. But somebody's got to pay for it. Somebody's got to go to work and earn the coppers.

'You see all these young sprogs, medallion men. They've three buttons missing off their shirt and a gold medallion hanging down. They specialize in getting heavily sunburned and worry, as though it's the end of the world, when the sunburn's fading away. I'd love to get one of them on top of a 200-foot chimney with all the muck coming up and going down his throat. He'd want to get back to the modern world, I can tell you.'

ONE MORNING in October 1985, a few weeks after his family returned from holiday, Fred went away early on his steamroller to open a solid fuel exhibition at Bury. When he got back in the evening Alison had gone with their three daughters, the Alsatian bitch and some of the furniture. The grandfather clock was still there; its tick echoed through the empty rooms. Reviewing events a few weeks later, Fred put on a brave front and spoke of the practicalities of living alone:

'I've managed all right. The cooking is a nuisance. You've got to stop whatever you're doing to go in and cook your dinner, and it takes a long time. I'm used to racing in and getting it down. As a variation to eggs and chips I bought one of those tin cans the size of a plate with a full dinner inside. Stuck it in the oven according to the instructions. It came out very well but it wasn't much of a helping so I had a tin of beans as well.

'I've got a new friend, Joe, who's been divorced for two years and he's given me some tips. When you have your tea you wash up immediately afterwards. You don't keep whizzing them in the sink or you end up with a great pile of dirty pots.

'He took me on my first trip to the supermarket. I felt a right berk shoving the trolley around. People kept looking at me. "That's him" sort of thing. God forbid that life should come to this – shoving a trolley round supermarkets.

Joe's brother's wife is a nice woman. She tells him to go off down to the pub while she gets on with all the jobs, decorating, joinery, the lot. You see her hard at it with the angle grinder and whatnot. She's taken both my pocket watches to the jeweller's and got them fettled up. I lost the end of my tie pin and she mended it. I should have married a bird like that.

'We've got lent to us, on sort of permanent loan, a brand-new automatic washing machine. We've had a bit of fun with that. We've not quite mastered how it works yet. We filled it up the other night with all the dirty jeans and gear, put the powder in, pressed the button – and nothing happened. After some groping we discovered that it was the fridge that was plugged into the socket, not the washing machine. We swapped the plug over and we got it going round. The wash came out quite well. We'd learned something. We knew what to do next time.

'It's very peaceful though, now we've got rid of the pop music that was on from 7 o'clock in the morning and all those young fellows who came round at night after the daughters. They filled the parlour. They broke the castors off the chaise longue. Six of them sat on it, big lads all six feet tall. There were times when I couldn't even sit in my own chair. I can recline now and play my Strauss waltzes with no opposition.

'A lady is coming to measure me up for some velvet curtains for the new bedroom. It's the top part of the extension intended to give us more living space, which ironically I've got far too much of now. But now I've gone so far with the job I'll finish it. I'll make it like a palace. The leaded windows are done. I've sanded the floor and I'll have a pleasant evening putting the sealer on.

'I've got a beautiful brass bedstead that I bought for a fiver and bulled up. It's a pity there's nobody to share its use.

'The picture I hung above it is a favourite of mine, painted about 1870, of a vista of spinning mills with black smoke rolling from the chimneys. Women then knew a bit about working. They all lived within 200 yards of the mills. They started at six o'clock in the morning and at eight had half an hour to go home for their breakfast. My mother did that at a bleach works. I don't think it did them any harm. She lasted till she was eighty.

'In Victorian times if you didn't work you were poor; there were no government handouts. England led the world and everybody had their nose down to the grindstone. All the tackle they had in the home was "handraulic": the mangle with big heavy wooden rollers, the broom for sweeping the carpets. Now there's more time for looking beautiful than ever because of all the modern equipment – washing machines, dishwashers, fancy cookers, microwaves. Even with a record machine you don't need to get up off your bum to make it go.

'There's this equal rights thing now. You never get women down the pit or at the top of a factory chimney, do you? No way. But they want half of everything. Difficult.

'Money was never really a problem between us. I didn't pocket all my wages. Alison had the chequebook. In my business I had a lucky start, first with the church jobs and then with the chimney jobs that followed, so early on I had a float of a couple of thousand in the bank which made me good for the credit I needed to take on really big jobs with public and private corporations and win a bit of a reputation where it's most helpful. But, even so, it's an up and down sort of job in more senses than one. When we made any money we spent it. Alison could have what she liked and I could have bits for my steam engine. We were often enough strapped for ready cash. Then along came television and made me notorious and all sorts of people rang up wanting me to do things. As I've said, the quality of life improved. But the pressure of it all got to Alison. She did the business arrangements and kept the books very well and she was content to live quietly without having all the extra load of arrangements thrust on her back. It enabled me to take it a bit easier on the chimney job but what has happened has happened, so it's back on the grafting again. I don't complain of that really. I still like going to work, I like the job. Alison used to say there was no living with me if I didn't have a chimney to climb, which is true – though it seems there's no living with me either way.

'Basically I'm a lonely man. Perhaps that's been part of the trouble, getting engrossed in my own things and not paying enough attention to the family. I suppose I could have taken them on holiday a bit more, but to me the steam engine rallies were a holiday. The kids used to enjoy it but they've grown up into young ladies and they don't want to play with steam engines any more. They prefer to go jigging about in discotheques, which I suppose is only natural. It's not everybody's idea of fun sitting in the living van of a steam engine in the middle of a wet field with a force nine gale blowing.

'One of the most alarming things about being left on my own is the number of letters and 'phone calls I've had from ladies volunteering to keep me company – as though I wasn't in enough trouble already.

'I had a letter from a lady in London who offered to come up and look after me. She claimed to be very interested in steam and said her greatest wish was to see my steam engine. Another claimed to be an authority on submarines. Some of them make unbelievable offers on the 'phone. "I just thought I'd give you a ring," one said, "because I'm feeling a bit low." My answer to that was, "So am I, love, at present."

'Then a lady I do actually know 'phoned. She said I needed looking after, which is true, but she also said I need somebody to drive me. What she meant by that I don't really know, but I don't take kindly to the prospect of being driven by anybody.

'I keep them all at bay. The safest course is to be a good lad till all the money matters are sorted out. I'm going to proceed with great caution.'

SHAM MISTRI, shopkeeper and friend, a man of Asian culture in whom family tradition ran strong, felt such concern at Fred's lonely state that he undertook a diplomatic mission to remedy it. One night, when Fred was passing a couple of hours working on his traction engine, Sham came down and bearded him in his engine shed.

'I can fix you up, Fred,' he announced, 'with a lady I know.'

'One of your staff?'

'That's right, yes. Are you interested?'

Fred couldn't afford to be interested but, not wishing to spurn good intentions, he asked what she was like.

'A good-looking lady,' Sham pronounced.

Fred raised a possible barrier. 'Would she like the world of old iron and Victoriana?'

'I am sure she would,' Sham asserted. 'She's been on her own a long time now, no commitments.'

Fred looked doubtful.

'Come down to my shop,' Sham urged, 'I'll fix you up. She works in the mornings, come in for some fags.'

'I've never done anything like this for a long time. It'd be very nerve-wracking.'

'She's a very nice lady.'

'She might not fancy an old bugger like me.'

Sham shrugged as though age was a trifle of no consequence.

'How old is she?' Fred asked with a trace of suspicion.

'No, Fred, she has never told me her age. But she will suit you. You will have to see her.'

'Not too young for an old boy like me?'

'You will be all right surely.'

'What is she interested in?'

'She likes dancing. I think she goes old-time dancing.'

Fred recoiled with horror.

'She has to find some interest, go somewhere,' Sham argued. 'She's got her own house, no commitments. I don't think she is looking for somebody to get married to. But the ball's in your court.'

'I don't really know, in my present situation. I don't even know if I want one around.'

'Look Fred, all I am doing is to introduce you to somebody to go out with, wash your clothes, make your breakfast.'

That sounded like a distinct improvement on old-time dancing, but by now Fred was beginning to master washing and breakfast-making. 'I'm managing OK myself,' he said.

'Well come and see me,' Sham invited. 'Never mind the lady, come and see me.'

Sensing something of a trap in the invitation Fred steered clear, but all this talk about possible new partners turned his thoughts in the autumn of 1985 to what kind of lady he might ideally like once the dust had settled:

'In the first place she'd have to be able to write. Alison was a good help to me. I could wander out and do what I wanted and she answered the 'phone and wrote everything down. I'm semi-literate. I only write down half of what's said and when I look at it three hours later I wonder what the hell it's all supposed to be about. Alison could suss people out and tell whether they were lunatics or not.

'For a start I wouldn't want a lady that might try to propel me into the modern world. You see them in the pub fascinated by some horrible racket coming out of the jukebox. I watched one pop celebrity on the telly. There was mass hysteria through the audience. All the women were jumping up and down. It looked and sounded bloody awful. No, I'd want somebody who was interested in antiques and steam engines and beautiful things. I wouldn't expect her to climb up chimneys or even to do anything in the steam department so long as she enjoyed the thing. I wouldn't want one that looks like a boiler, but she wouldn't have to be beautiful. I would want her to like beautiful clothes. I can be scruffy, but I want my lady to look beautiful. Alison looked very good when she was toffed up. I like nice dresses, preferably ones that fit, black nylons and high heeled shoes, which I think enhance a lady's legs, make 'em look nice. Half the tackle Alison had, I picked. Most of her best frocks were black 'uns.

'I really like the period clothes you see on the television. They wore some beautiful tackle. Some of the dresses were magnificent. It makes you wonder what they've got underneath. You don't have to wonder now. You can see it all straight away. No mystery left.

'In practical terms I need a lady who'd keep me on the straight and narrow. I'm prone to run a bit wild every now and again. I need a sobering, steadying influence. I'd want her to keep me out of the ale house and shout at me for excessive smoking. I know the fags are doing me harm and I'll go the same way as my father who coughed himself to death. But my nervous system's in such a state I really can't stop. I'm a drug addict, which I'm ashamed of.

'I know you can't ask for everything in one woman. Basically she'd have to like the world of Queen Victoria and be able to answer the telephone and be a bit diplomatic with people who ring up and want me to do all sorts of unbelievable things – to have enough sense to suss the nutcases out from the genuine ones and get it all written down on a piece of paper. That's the essential thing. I need somebody capable of writing.

'Really I've been harassed much more by the media than by women. I know they're only doing their job drumming up stories, but it's wearing when you've trouble on your mind. I've lost a stone in two months. Newspaper men spent all morning lying in wait at the bottom of a spire I was mending. 'Just a word, Mr Dibnah," they kept shouting. I shouted back words that were unprintable. "Go away," words to that effect. It was quite funny. "Mr Dibnah had no comment to make," they wrote in the paper. They daren't have put down what I really said.

One thing I've learned about journalists is that they ring you up and appear to be very friendly when they're really trying to get you to say something they can make a mess of and make you look a right wally. Just before Alison left, some television people we didn't know rang up and asked me if I was doing anything interesting with my steam engine. As it happened I was. I was going to Wigan with it. "Oo, sounds interesting," they said and arrived at the door. It instantly became clear that their goal was to get us to talk about the impending divorce, not about the steam engine at all.

'Most of the media people have been quite pleasant most of the time. I can't say I had any hard trips out of them. If you don't tell lies you can't go far wrong. When you invent things and then try to remember what you've said, that's when you drop a clanger.'

THE BIGGEST sum raised towards financing the divorce came from mortgaging the house. Fred had never had a mortgage and it made him uncomfortable. And that was not the end of it. Other things would have to go, not his steam engines – that would have been the end of the world – but a slightly less-prized vehicle, his 1927 AJS 350 cc motorcycle. For the last time he put it together and polished it up.

'This a very sad occasion. The same machine with an overhead valve engine, but with nothing else different, won the Isle of Man TT about 1924. Those were the days when England made the best motorcycles in the world. Not so any more.

'I bought it for twenty quid after I came out of the army and did it up – stove enamelled and nickel-plated it. I thought I'd made a good job of it till I saw what a mate of mine, Alan

Crompton, had done with a 1921 Sunbeam. It took my breath away. Everything gleamed. You could see your face in the crankcase. He won all the prizes in the *concours d'élégance* at all the top motorcycle shows. It took him a week to clean it before he went.

'Mine was a bit more of a workhorse. I went to work on it for ten years. Once, in midwinter, I went to Leeds over Blackstone Edge and arrived with my hands frozen to the handlebars.

'It's taken a back seat since I got the steamroller and a family. It's stayed in the shed in pieces. When I'd put it together again I had my first outing on it since I laid it up after renovating it in 1969. Riding it again filled me with nostalgia and it was quite frightening too, zooming along at sixty with the wind rushing through what's left of my hair. I felt like keeping it but there again these days you'd have to wear one of those plastic helmets and I'm not into that sort of thing. I've always known it's worth a bob or two, so now I'm desperate for money it'll have to go to the auction. If we get two lunatics bidding against each other it might raise a couple of grand.'

THE LUNATICS didn't turn up and the bike didn't quite make that money. It was knocked down for £1,700 'to a man from Macclesfield,' said Fred, 'who'll give it a good home. I'll have to weigh the proceeds into the building society for the war effort.'

All this really was superficial, putting a brave face on things, easing the pain with a few jokes. Looking back a few years later, Fred remembered it as far the blackest time of his life:

'The most terrifying thing was waking at four o'clock in the morning with not a sound in the house except the beat of the grandfather clock. I'd get up and bang the wireless on as soon as they started broadcasting. I'd mess about, doing nothing, picking things up and putting them down, until dawn came and it was time to go to work.

'Joe, the other divorced man who helped me with the shopping, drank with me at night. We tried to drown our sorrows, but usually we finished up at the point of tears. I got enough ale down to put me to sleep – enough in ordinary times to have kept me under till ten o'clock in the morning – but no matter how much I drank I woke at four and couldn't go back to sleep again.

'I began to hate the thought of coming home from work or getting back from the pub. I'd never been all alone before. I lived with my mam and dad until I was twenty-nine. I know now what my mother meant as a widow, rebuking me for not visiting her more often: "You don't know what it's like on your own, nobody to talk to, day or night." She was right. I didn't, but I do now. Even if you don't talk there's a comfort, a sort of companionship, in just hearing somebody moving about the place. I still had the things I loved, the steam engines and the antiques and the grandfather clock. It didn't help. The place felt totally empty.

'I've always called myself a loner. I realize now that I'm not.

'People would say by way of comfort: "You'll get over it." You do in the end but it's a bitter blow. There's a long time of misery and depression. The only winners in a divorce are the lawyers. I'd shoot myself before I'd go through it again.'

WHAT MOST helped Fred through the bad days was work. His enthusiasm for the new extension he was building understandably waned for lack of occupants, but he got more work done on his traction engine and, when it was clear that Alison would not come back, he went through the sad ceremony of changing the plate on the steamroller that bore her name. He renamed it Betsy after his mother, which seemed good for all time. As he said, wives may change but mothers are forever.

Fred also just about completed his steam-driven workshop. Backed by high trees, it extended across the whole 130-foot length of his backyard. The enlarged engine shed housed both the roller and the tractor and all the Victorian power tools Fred had resurrected from scrap.

Funnels puffed, pistons reciprocated, shafts turned, pulleys revolved, leather belting flapped. At one end of the yard a circular saw whistled through wood to feed the boiler; at the other a stone saw screamed out iridescent fantails of flying spray.

Steam enthusiasts, some from abroad, came on pilgrimage and watched in pious awe. But from some of those in daily earshot of the workshop murmurs of complaint continued to be heard and there was some investigation by council officials.

'I think the council understand me,' Fred concluded. 'They send school parties down to learn something about the marvellous world that passed before they were born. It's obviously seen as a valuable contribution to the heritage and also to the environment and conservation.

'As I've said before, I'm doing no harm to the birds. There are plenty of nests in the surrounding trees. The steam keeps them warm. Owls live in the engine shed and little wrens. It's home for them. You could regard it as a sort of nature reserve.'

Not all the neighbours took quite that view. Occasionally some retaliated with counterblasts on electric guitars and motorcycle engines. One man remonstrated by throwing blocks of concrete into the yard. But protest was sporadic. In general Fred was left in peace to contemplate his treasure house of revolving ironmongery and to reflect that if only this survived him he would not have lived in vain.

The steeplejacking was going well. A bigger proportion of the jobs than usual were for repair, not demolition. Fred saved one chimney by interceding with the owner:

'He rang me up and asked me to give him a price to knock it down. I'd admired that chimney since I was a child. It's a handsome-looking thing with an ornamental top made of cast iron in big segments bolted together, a beautiful piece of workmanship. He argued that it served no purpose, which from a utilitarian point of view was true. It never had a lot of smoke up it. The engine disappeared before the Second World War and it's stood there as a monument for nearly sixty years. But I loved it, so I pointed out that it had his name in pot letters down the side – a perfect free advert.

'"But that's no good,' he said, "facing into the town. If we kept it do you think you could turn it round to face the new motorway?"'

Fred had to confess that revolving a standing chimney round was beyond his many skills, but he wouldn't be drawn into knocking it down. He kept out of the owner's sight and put him off whenever he called on the telephone.

'Then one day he nobbled us when we were buying downspouts in a yard opposite. He was up there banging on his office window and we couldn't escape. We agreed to go just as far as putting ladders up to make an inspection. When we came down of course we reported that it was basically very sound indeed. He still wouldn't agree to mending it. He insisted he wanted it knocked down.

'I played for time. I prevaricated and made excuses till he retired because I'd heard a buzz that his son was in favour of preserving the chimney. I think he first had the big boys round from Manchester because I'd got in the habit of being hard to catch, but they scared him a bit with the money and I agreed to take the job on for a very humble fee. I'd have done it for nowt if he'd pressed me.'

Fred had a happy week or two on the chimney. The weather was fine. The mortar in the repointing set quickly. He painted the lettering up the side and the cast iron ornamental top. The job completed, he sat at peace high up on the scaffolding, back against the sun-warmed wall of the chimney.

'It's a beautiful pile of bricks,' he said. 'It'll last for ever. It'll see us all out.'

An airship floated by quite close, a reminder, like the renovated chimney at his back, of happier days gone by.

The weather stayed good. Business boomed. Another nice job came up, for the repair of an unusual chimney, octagonal in section. It belonged to Courtaulds and as Fred came down the ladders from making his inspection the manager, Mr Greenhalgh, waited in the yard, fearing the worst.

Fred obligingly confirmed it. 'The good brick at the top is rocking about in the wind and cracking up the old brickwork. There are a lot of new cracks. You can tell they're new because instead of being dirty and full of soot like the old ones they're a nice clean pink, which is a nasty sign, bad news.'

'What's the remedy?'

'The only remedy is one-inch diameter iron rods tightened into cast iron corner pieces to hold the eight corners together, and prevent them from spreading outwards.'

'And that'll hold it?'

'Oh aye. Iron bands'd hold a pack of dominoes together. Have it by the what's it.'

'How long would that last?'

'Put it this way.' said Fred. 'Me and thee won't be round. It'll outlast us all right. The thing is to get a grip of it before it gets a grip of you.'

'How much?'

'Two grand.'

Mr Greenhalgh looked solemn.

'It seems a lot,' Fred conceded, 'but there's a lot of engineering involved in the job. Them that built it were not good wi' t' ruler. All those eight sides are a different size.'

'Two thousand pounds needs some finding.'

'Hold a raffle,' Fred suggested.

They raised the money somehow and Fred enjoyed some pleasant autumn days, floating round the chimney in his bosun's chair. But in the evening his thoughts turned to darker themes.

'If every day were like these days it'd be beautiful, this job. It's not so pleasant when the wind's howling and the paint's blowing off the edge of the brush all over your specs. God forbid, another seventeen years of that to pay off the divorce settlement. I was nearly ready for retiring – well, not retiring, I'll never retire, I'll die doing something – but at least having life a bit easier. I'm getting old and it's a young man's job, climbing chimneys.'

At the next place they didn't consider holding a raffle to pay for the chimney repair, but they did run a competition.

It was a demolition job. The chimney was too closely surrounded by buildings to be felled. It would be knocked down brick by brick. Because of the competition Fred found out for the first time in his life how many bricks he would have to throw down to demolish a chimney.

Weighing up the job in the yard with Bob Stones, the manager, he suggested lowering the chimney not all the way to the ground but only to the height of surrounding buildings, leaving a stump that would be roofed over. That would reduce the estimate quite considerably – from £8,000 to £6,500 – because chimney walls are much thicker at the bottom and need more shifting.

Fred confessed that he was keen to get the job. 'Winter's coming. It's near home. It'll be a good job in bad weather because, unlike pointing and painting, it's not affected by the rain.'

He had just come from a pointing job where twice, just as he finished, rainstorms had washed the wet mortar away. The third time he was lucky but, for the present, he wasn't looking for any more pointing jobs.

The competition among employees was to guess the number of bricks in the chimney which would be patiently counted as Fred threw them down. Estimates varied from several hundred to two million.

Donald Paiton, Fred's assistant, got Fred to measure the chimney and spent a day and a half calculating the number of bricks. Fred promptly forgot the number – 'twenty-odd thousand, something like that,' he thought. He wasn't eligible to enter the competition and was unattracted in any case by the prize, a weekend for two in Paris.

Paris, like Greece, was abroad, but on reflection not quite as bad. It had one redeeming feature – the Eiffel tower. 'It's nine hundred and something feet high. I wouldn't mind to have a do at climbing that.'

His next climb was a more modest one, up the spire of Harwood church on the edge of the town, in sight of the moors. 'A nice peaceful job,' Fred said. 'At least I'm doing something that has some chance of surviving. They don't knock 'em all down.'

At the base of the spire he discovered initials cut by the workers who had built it. Fred felt for them. 'The blokes who built this particular church must have had a hell of a battle. It's built on a kind of rock that's terrible to chop, it's as hard as iron. They must have had big muscles. If you get a hammer and chisel and start clouting at this sort of rock you're worn out after an hour or two. They must have done it all day long.'

Fred pointed the spire and braced it with steel rods, and he secured the three hundredweight stone cross at the top which had been rocking in the wind.

The churchwarden, Fred Rogerson, an old friend who had worked fifty years in the spinning mills, came round to inspect.

'Is it solid now?' he shouted up.

Fred performed a pantomime of trying in vain to shake the cross. 'It'll be here when we're all dead.'

'A couple of hundred years?'

'Easy. It'll never fall down.'

But there was some bad news too. Fred descended to the bell tower where the four stone pillars had rotted. 'If you were up here with me you could pull lumps out with your hand.'

'There's no danger I'd be up there with thee,' Mr Rogerson shouted, bringing into play the opera glasses he had brought to spare such an ascent.

Fred dislodged a handful of stone from one of the pillars.

'Could they not be repaired?' Mr Rogerson shouted.

'You can bodge 'em up with sand and cement, but in twenty years they'll be as bad again.'

He tossed a small shower of broken stone at the church warden's feet. 'We should try to get four new 'uns as cheap as we can. There's cracks in all of them. They're buggered.'

Mr Rogerson stepped back from the bouncing stones and gracefully accepted Fred's advice. He lowered his opera glasses, stood erect and formally proclaimed:

'I have the authority of the standing committee to proceed.'

Fred made a good job of it. The new pillars shone cleanly against the dark stone of the bell tower. Everybody was pleased. Then when Fred went back to collect his tackle, an appalling thing had happened. The graveyard looked as though it had been shelled. Twenty-four of the most beautiful gravestones had been knocked over and smashed to pieces.

Fred was appalled. 'We've had these vandals round before. They've broken numerous leaded windows which the poor people of the church had replaced after they were broken once before and they've climbed the lightning conductor and cut 400 feet of my rope to shreds. They've done more than ten thousand pounds' worth of damage. What sort of people can do that, smash to pieces beautiful marble crosses that have stood there for a hundred years?'

Fred answered his own question in sorrow, indignation and anger:

'They were evidently more than children to be able to shove over stones of that weight. They must be in the early stages of manhood. Some of 'em no doubt are out of work. They're very unhappy and they have a grudge against society as we used to know it, all nice and peaceful. They just want to disrupt everything they can lay their just want to hands on.

'Why have we gone like this? Things were really bad in the 1930s. People were actually hungry then. None of these people are hungry. Yet those fellows in the 1930s didn't do this sort of thing.

'They knew that if they did wrong they'd be in trouble. Now they've no need to fear anything. We've gone too soft. "Poor little Johnny, he couldn't help it, he's under a lot of stress" – and that sort of thing. I mean, the old Ayatollah, if you pinch a loaf of bread there, bang, it's the old finger off I think if they did a bit of that here things would be straighter.

'From what I've read in the papers I believe that when they had the birch in the Isle of Man vandalism was practically non-existent. Now, with the bloody wonderful Common Market job, they've had to stop using it. It'll never get better until they fire 'em into line – National Service or something like that. There are all these arguments against it but the people who put them forward never come up with a solution, do they? Never. It just goes steadily worse day by day.

'What can you do? There's a lot to be said for the olden days and how they did things. They were better craftsmen, better at everything. They had respect for property. Now they've no respect for anything. All they want is a life of bloody pleasure.'

NEAR MISS

FROM THE beginning, Harry Forshaw, the demolition contractor who often hires Fred, was worried about the chimney at Oldham.

He had nearly finished knocking down the mill, which left a flattened area almost the size of a football pitch to topple the chimney into. On the left side stood an electricity sub-station, on the right a row of modern houses occupied by old people. The flattened area between was large enough to allow a reasonable margin of error. But behind the chimney, on the opposite side from where it should be made to fall, were avenues of semi-detached houses. The nearest of them was only 12 yards from the base of the chimney. If it went completely the wrong way scores of homes would be reduced to rubble.

That was what troubled Harry Forshaw. He and Fred stood together outside the houses looking up at the chimney.

'None of these people need have any anxiety,' Fred assured him. 'How many chimneys have you seen jump backwards? None.'

'Thirty-six feet is very close,' Harry brooded. He'd had a feeling all along for the less hazardous method of demolishing the chimney brick by brick. Fred was keen to escape the tedium of that job.

'Look,' Fred offered, 'when the chimney falls I'll stand my ground between it and the nearest house.'

Harry, a big, bearded man of gentle manners, looked no happier. If the houses were buried under the chimney it would help in no way to have Fred buried with them.

'We've done 'em in tighter places than this,' Fred asserted, and passed on to the aspect that really bothered him.

'The insurance people want £3,000 premium before I knock out a brick. It's not right. Those men have carpets a foot thick and Mark 10 jaguars.'

This did nothing to cheer Harry up. If the insurance company wanted £3,000 premium, the job could hardly be as risk-free as Fred represented it. Faces appeared at the windows of the houses, anxious ears pricked.

Fred has two *bêtes noires*: insurers and expensive motorcars.

'I can't find £3,000 for those men in my present straitened state. I've never done any damage,' he asserted forcefully if not quite accurately. 'It wouldn't be so bad if I'd smashed things up all over the place.'

The faces in the windows winced. Harry looked glum.

'I've never done any damage,' Fred insisted again, clearly believing it for the moment. 'That's what upsets me most of all.'

'I suppose looking at it as they might, it looks very dodgy,' Harry suggested.

'Well, they're timid. It's the old thing – stick the compasses in the map at the centre of the chimney, a radius of one-and-half-times the height of the chimney and everything inside that circle is dead in their eyes.'

The faces in the windows went pale.

'I suppose it's up to the insurance whether the job goes on or not,' Harry said.

'It's a ridiculous amount.'

'It'd cost a lot more, I suppose, if you had to demolish it a brick at a time by hand.'

Fred dismissed that unwelcome subject 'No, we must drop it. It'll be one to get the adrenalin going.'

He moved off in a burst of laughter, in which neither Harry nor the faces in the windows joined.

The insurance business came to what Fred considered a 'happy conclusion'. He got the premium down to £700, and now in a less combative mood he retreated a short step from absolute certainty. 'I'm ninety-nine per cent confident,' he modestly told anybody who cared to listen.

He started work on preparing the chimney for felling.

Passing residents came up and bearded Fred. They brought up reports that he had recently buried a car under one of his chimneys. Fred reassured them. It might have looked like a catastrophe, he conceded, but was in fact a deliberate joke:

'One Sunday we were about to drop a chimney with a beautiful-looking car parked right in the firing line. A crowd gathered, as usual, hoping to see a disaster. This time they thought they'd get lucky. "That car's in the way," they murmured. "He's going to hit it."

'Several of the more conscientious came forward and pointed it out to me. I thanked them but pressed on with my helpers building the pyre. People started shouting out about the car. As the fire took hold great murmurs of scandalized anxiety passed through the onlookers. "Is he blind? He should be stopped. Can't he see he's going to wreck that car?"

'Then, boom, down the chimney came. Flattened the car completely. There was a groan of horror and all kinds of shouted rebukes. "You wouldn't be told. You've done it now. That'll cost you a bob or two."

'In fact I did it, as you might say, by appointment. I'd noticed the car parked in a risky spot when I first arrived and I went down and spoke to a bird who flushed out the owner. I asked him to shift it. "No," he said, "It's had it, it's buggered."

'It was too. From a distance it looked quite good. The windows were clean, tyres were up, paintwork shining. But close up you could see it was full of pitholes. It was one that had been lovingly cared for on the outside but nothing done underneath. "I want to get rid of it," the owner said, "but nobody'll have it. I've rung three scrap chaps but none of them has turned up."

'So I volunteered to see it off for him. We towed it even more central to the line of fire, and that's what the spectators saw, what appalled them when it disappeared under the heavy stone that the chimney was made of.

'It was a sound job. The car was so completely flattened that it made not the slightest bump in the profile of the heap of stone that fell on it. When we shifted the stone we found the car had been flattened to four inches thick, even the engine. It's the best job I ever did on a motorcar.'

ON THE Friday when the last bricks were cut out and the last pit props hammered into the gap Harry Forshaw made a tour of the closer houses, ringing and rat-tatting on doors to ask residents to evacuate the premises shortly before 11 o'clock on Sunday morning when the chimney was due to be felled.

A middle-aged lady took it in with evident surprise. 'Oh?' she responded in a querying tone.

'You've nothing to worry about,' Harry reassured her, having evidently overcome his own worry. 'Nothing's ever gone wrong before.'

'Does that mean it isn't entirely safe?' an old woman at the next house asked, getting to the nub of the matter.

Harry skated round it. 'There'll be no problem. Fred's very competent at doing his job.'

'Yes,' the lady said doubtfully, wishing to cast no aspersions but well aware that the question had not quite been answered.

'He's had no accidents as yet.'

Harry warmed to his theme and produced variants of assurance as his tour proceeded. 'He's done them in worse places than this,' he told an old man. 'He'll send it that way.' Harry indicated a line of descent quite opposite from where they were standing.

It all went without too much backbiting until he encountered a bald man of sharp intelligence wearing a smart cardigan.

'Is it going to be safe?' the man asked.

Harry went as close as he truthfully could to saying it would be.

'Because we've got an old lady of ninety-two inside. She can't walk. We can't get her out. What'd be the danger if we stayed?'

Harry wasn't to be drawn on that one. 'I don't think you'll be allowed to stay,' he said. 'The factory inspector wouldn't allow it.'

'The fact is,' the man said, hammering it home, 'that it might just fall this way.'

'There'll be no danger. Nothing's ever gone wrong.'

'There's always a first time,' the man said. It then occurred to him that it wouldn't be the first time. 'I believe there was one at the corner of Drury Lane that actually killed a woman.'

This was the furthest any of the residents went in disputing the right of anybody to imperil their home or a factory inspector to have them ordered out.

The last old lady visited seemed to harbour a hidden reluctance Harry found difficult to overcome.

'There's no danger to your premises,' he said, coming up with another variant. 'It's just a precaution to be on the safe side.'

She looked troubled.

'Your home'll be all right,' Harry assured her.

It had no effect. Her home wasn't what was bothering her. 'It's very disappointing,' she said. 'Can't we stay and watch it through the window?'

Harry was relieved, after his hour of truth-economizing diplomacy, to return to his natural frankness. 'You're in reach of the chimney,' he said.

She looked rueful. 'We've all been looking forward to seeing it through the window. We thought it'd be a novelty.'

Sunday arrived. From the foot of the chimney Fred looked out across the demolished area and spotted a giant crane which had been moved into the extreme far corner. He took offence. 'Has your driver no confidence in us?' he demanded of Harry Forshaw. 'Look how far away he's parked that crane.'

'Chimney enthusiasts came out from wherever they lurked between fellings and helped to build the bonfire against the pit props at the foot of the chimney. A rowdy contingent of the Fred Dibnah Appreciation Society arrived from Halifax and got stuck in with the wood and tyres.

Fred moved amongst them, shifting something here on the pyre and asking for something to be dropped there. He found he had come without the old motor horn which he uses to signal the imminent collapse of a chimney. He borrowed a policeman's whistle.

A crowd of some thousands was forming like a football crowd round the demolished rectangle out of the reach of the chimney. The residents on whom Harry had served notice to quit for half an hour compliantly left their homes, most of them formally dressed for the occasion. The old lady of ninety-two was bumped down the steps in a wheelchair and hoisted into the back seat of a car.

Fred waved his helpers away and scattered paraffin over the bonfire. Some police moved on people who crept in to watch from the side streets within possible range. Others went from door to door and walked through entries into the small back gardens to make sure everybody had gone.

The fire did not start well. The young girl, who had been given the honour of applying the blazing torch at 11 o'clock by Fred's pocket watch, could make no impression. Fred himself got the fire to splutter and then to blaze. A dense black cloud of smoke from the burning tyres rolled out of the chimney top. The wind carried it almost horizontal above the house tops and the main road to Manchester. The crowd of watchers on the far side of the demolished area became invisible in the haze.

These were anxious moments. Fred had done his work, carefully taking into account all known factors. Others were unknown. Nobody could know what weaknesses had developed in an old chimney that might distort the fall and cause it to go the wrong way. It was even possible that the props might burn away and the chimney, against calculations, remain standing on its remaining base. That had happened once before. The remedy was more dangerous than defusing a bomb. It required Fred to work at the base of the chimney, knocking out more bricks and hoping to escape at the first rumblings of the fall. It was not a performance he cared to repeat.

The fire burned. The smoke cloud turned paler after the consumption of the tyres. Flames shot from the chimney top.

There was nothing visibly wrong but Fred had a certain foreboding. He prowled round the fire. He crouched at the back where the movement of a rod he had inserted would indicate when the weight of the chimney was beginning to settle forward.

The rod wasn't moving, though by now it should have been. The one helper who stayed with him lit two cigarettes and stuck one in Fred's mouth. It waggled as he spoke. He rose, worried, prowled round the side again and returned to the back. 'What's holding it?' he complained.

The chimney did not pitch, or very little. With a rumbling roar it settled down almost on its own base. Everyone close by ran. Bouncing bricks pursued Fred, chimney enthusiasts, appreciation society delegates and camera crew. Clouds of soot and mortar dust darkened the day.

Miraculously nobody was hurt. None of the houses was damaged. Everybody was frightened and relieved. The older chimney enthusiasts sat down on wall tops, solemnly staring at the broken bricks that littered the road. The chairman of the appreciation society in a bright anorak clapped Fred on the back. 'Bloody marvellous, lad,' he bawled.

Fred had lost or swallowed his cigarette. Somebody gave him another. Several passed lights under his nose aimed at the shaking end of the cigarette.

'My nerves haven't come back right,' he apologized.

He spotted a small tree that had been growing near the base of the chimney. 'Didn't I say I wouldn't damage that?'

'Bloody marvellous, lad,' the appreciation society chairman shouted.

The chimney enthusiasts sitting on the wall tops, aloof from the emotion, held a quiet technical inquest. They concluded that an area of weakness must have developed over the years in the back wall of the chimney, the side, that is, opposite the one in which the gap was cut. They figured that when the props burned away the chimney started to keel forward but the weakened area at the back had rapidly collapsed with the initial movement, causing the chimney not to pitch forward, as it should, but to settle down vertically on its base.

'You forgot to blow your whistle,' somebody from the appreciation society shouted. His fellow members roared with laughter.

Fred found the police whistle still in his fist. He passed it to a policewoman.

'Do you not need it any more?' she asked.

'No,' said Fred. 'It's all over with for today.'

Boys had been shoving paper at him to sign autographs. He seemed too dazed to notice them, but then he suddenly seized one and signed. 'Take that to the chemist's. He'll give you a prescription.'

Fred laughed at his own joke, took some little dancing steps away from the crowd and wandered alone for a moment among the fallen bricks.

He came face to face with a sympathetic-looking young woman whom he began to remember having invited to the felling. This was Sue Lorenz whom, some time later, he married.

RE-MARRIAGE AND REFORM

IN 1986 Fred was nearing fifty and facing the prospect of a bleak old age with only his steam engines for company. Sue was twenty years younger. From the beginning they had something in common. Both were divorced and both were interested in steam.

'I'd seen him around,' Sue remembered, 'but we first met at a big steam rally in Cheshire where I was camping with friends. It was in the middle of the divorce proceedings and Fred was in a bad way. He was sad and miserable, quite a pathetic sort of figure and very drunk, too. I don't think he remembered inviting us to the Oldham chimney. But he was stone cold sober when he came to do the job and it was no fault of his that it came down the wrong way and nearly finished the lot of us off.'

'I suppose you could say it cemented our friendship,' Fred commented. 'I had a bit of a chat with her in the pub afterwards and we went out for a meal, I think. I was impressed, at her flat, with her collection of books. They were about architecture and antiques and canals, which revealed to me a sound kind of person.'

Sufficiently sound to be offered a close view of his engines and a tour of his backyard steam workshop. In his loneliest days Fred had never weakened in his determination that any woman he took up with would be required to show an intelligent interest in it. Sue passed the test

'Shortly afterwards Fred rang me up to give him a bit of support. He was going to Halifax to speak to the Fred Dibnah Appreciation Society. It was in a little pub and there were lots of men waiting, all similar to Fred, wearing flat caps and smoking Woodbines.'

The appreciation society had always been rowdy. This night they exceeded themselves.

'Some of them were respectable businessmen in the daytime,' Fred remembered, 'Round Table sort of people. But that didn't hold them back when they got the ale down. They went on into the early hours. I woke up in the middle of the night to a terrible row. Everybody was hopelessly drunk. They were throwing things at each other and the projectiles were going through windows. It sounded as though there was a war on. When we got up all the windows were broken down below. I'll never forget that as long as I live.'

Shortly afterwards the Fred Dibnah Appreciation Society disbanded.

Sue believes that at the time, living alone, Fred was coping better than he suggests.

'He'd got himself into a little routine of going shopping once a week with another divorced man and he was actually making an effort to cook a decent meal at night. Ironing flummoxed him. He did a deal one day with a fairground man. Fred agreed to switch on the lights of their Christmas tree if somebody would iron him a shirt to do an after-dinner talk in. He wouldn't try to work the washing machine. His friend was allowed to do his washing in Fred's machine provided he did Fred's as well. Buying clothes he just never did. To this day he won't go to the shops to buy anything for himself. I have to go and choose for him.'

She moved in. They planned to get married at a steam rally during the summer. 'But,' says Sue, 'the Press got the notion that there was something going on in Fred's life that the world ought to know about. They camped outside the door and chased us around. They so much interfered with life that we decided to put an end to it by bringing our marriage forward.'

But before that, on a day of snow squalls, they levelled matters with one of the newshounds.

'The most forceful of them,' Fred recalled, 'was this reporter guy wearing a light mac with big lapels like an American gangster. "All we want,' he said, "is a picture of you and your new lady friend together, then we'll go." It was a sort of blackmail.'

Sue, to Fred's surprise, agreed. 'We'll do it,' she said, 'but at the top of the chimney.'

'Great,' the American-style reporter shouted. 'Brilliant. Magic.'

He accepted the offer without troubling to consult his photographer, who would have the job of climbing up through whistling snow. The poor man was about to embark, as Fred said, on 'a very worrying period of his life'.

Sue had not been up a chimney before, and it was not the best of days for anybody's first attempt. But she got into her jeans and boots and climbed to the scaffolding 150 feet up.

The photographer needed longer for his preparations. He took a long time at the bottom, according to Sue, 'dancing about, adjusting his trousers and his coat and his camera and his hat and gloves. He started slowly and halfway up came almost to a complete halt.'

Fred went down to him and, in something of an acrobatic feat, got down past him on the ladder, so he was able to offer some moral support and advice from the rungs immediately below. Thus encouraged, the photographer eventually reached the scaffolding. But, once there, he wasn't fit to stand. He lay full length on the boards, sweating while the snow settled on him.

He wasn't much of a climber, but he proved to be a man of courage and tenacity. Fred offered to get him safely down.

'No, no,' he said. 'I'll be all right. just give me a minute or two.'

They waited. He rose, tried a snap or two, then paused to

give himself a breather. Some composure was returning. To make a little light conversation Sue asked him if he could feel the chimney swaying in the wind.

It wasn't intended to put him off – all chimneys sway in the wind – but it did. He went pale. Determined to make a last desperate effort to do his duty, he fired off a few snaps, then asked to go down.

The newspaper did not use any of the pictures. There was too much camera shake.

That episode put paid to some of the press harassment. Their marriage early in 1987 killed off the interest altogether. It also made Fred feel more comfortable.

'I'm a great believer in the Victorian state of affairs and I didn't like this living over the brush. I think Sue wanted to marry me as much as I wanted to marry her, so the sooner the better, I suppose.'

Sue had already made a start on Fred's house training. Now she embarked on a programme of reform which was to develop on several fronts with the passing years. In a surprising first move she asked him to grow a moustache.

'I've always thought men with moustaches must be quite vain,' Fred said. 'I've never needed a moustache or a beard to hide behind or hair on my head to hide under. It was an unexpected request but I thought I'd have a go if it pleased her.'

'It was perhaps part of a master plan,' Sue revealed, 'to make it different here. It's very difficult moving into somebody else's house and I wanted to change something, not to change Fred but just to change his visual image a little bit, make him look a bit different.'

Fred was beginning to look a bit different as required – then one day his moustache came to grief. 'I was having a scrub up after work. Got the razor out with a flourish and before I knew it I'd shaved half the thing off. I'd only got one half still on and that was the end of that attempt. I had to shave it all off and have a fresh start.'

The moustache was only the beginning. 'He had some really bad traits and I told him that if I was going to stay he would have to change. We had tremendous battles.'

Fred's fluent and amusing talk, which has won him admiration nationwide, was something, Sue decided, that people could have too much of.

'He was terribly self-centred and thoughtless. We'd go into a pub and he'd be so busy talking about himself he'd just not notice when his turn came to get his money out and buy a round.

'The other things that upset me were his excessive drinking and smoking. He used to go on great drinking sessions and then spend the next day in bed recovering from these mammoth bouts. The first thing was to get rid of the hangers-on who used to take him off to the pub and perhaps quite enjoyed seeing him so drunk that he was scarcely capable of getting himself home. I realize that he does sometimes need to drink to release the tensions of work but I think he was creating more tensions by drinking, because he then spent the next day worrying because he was unfit to go to work.

'I have got him to moderate his drinking, at least on week nights. He gets by with a couple of bottles of Guinness drunk at the fireside. But smoking has been a complete triumph. He's cut it out completely. I was so worried for him that I kept on and on about it. Then one day of his own free will he said he was going to give up.'

There were several positive factors in giving up cigarettes, not least that Fred didn't really want to smoke. He resented the cost and the annoyance of running out – especially if it happened at the top of a chimney and involved the time and inconvenience of hauling up cigarettes and matches tied in a rope. Above all, he despised himself for his addiction.

Fred's smoking had increased during his time alone. His new marriage made him take stock. 'I really was a bag of nerves, smoking fifty cigarettes a day. I was gasping and my heart was going like a steam hammer when I climbed a chimney. My voice, as I heard listening to some old recordings the other day, had become a half-strangulated croak. I realized that Sue's a lot younger than me and that I'd have to keep myself in much better nick.'

His mother had been at him for years, sighing as he smoked three or four cigarettes in the course of a short visit and reminding him of the fate of his father, who departed at the end of a life-long trail of cigarette smoke.

'I used to think it was all right for her, sitting there retired with a fire halfway up the chimney. She didn't have domestic dissension or money troubles to put up with. It was worry as much as anything that kept me smoking so heavily.

'Sue helped in the first place by tackling the worry habit head on. We'd discuss in a rational way what bothered me, usually money, and then she'd say, "Right, we've talked it over, forget about it now. Worrying'll do no good. You'll only make yourself ill." I learned to worry a lot less. I didn't feel under such pressure. I became more patient with people, a lot more relaxed.'

At the same time Sue kept up the harassing attack Fred's mother had practised. 'Whenever I lit up she was after me, repeating like a parrot: "You've only just put one out, you've only just put one out."

The campaign no doubt had its effect but it was an unforeseeable event, an early morning downpour, that brought Fred to the point of giving up. En route to Haydock Park with his steamroller, he had parked overnight in a lay-by on the East Lancashire road. He slept in the living van. In the morning rain was drumming on the roof and cascading down the van's windows. By long habit Fred reached under the bed for his cigarettes. The packet was empty. He groped among the supplies Sue had put up for him. There were no cigarettes.

Head down against the driving rain, drenched by spray thrown up by the traffic, Fred trudged a quarter of a mile to a newsagent's shop. The shop, the traffic, the road had become by then a wavering watery vision. As Fred said, 'You don't know what rain is until you have to wear specs.'

He smoked two cigarettes, soggy and disintegrating, on the way back and arrived at the van wet through to the skin.

'I thought: "I must be crazy. I'll never do this again as long as I live." I smoked the rest of the packet during the weekend, but made a real effort at giving up on the Monday. I got through to twelve noon before I succumbed and went for another packet. It doesn't sound a very heroic achievement, but in all my working life I'd never before gone a full morning without smoking.

Sue encouraged him with lavish praise.

'I cut down stage by stage. First, I repeated my performance of getting to the end of the morning before I had a smoke, then till late afternoon, then I'd go a whole day without.'

'When he came home.' said Sue, 'I used to ask him, "Have you had a cigarette today?" If he said he hadn't I'd give him little presents to encourage him and make him feel as though he'd done well.'

This somewhat nursery-like approach was helpful but maybe provoked some rebellion deep in Fred's macho soul.

'I had a relapse. I went to look at a chimney stack at Great Harwood, near Blackburn, and the demolition man got out of his car with two cigarettes in his mouth and one of those American flamethrower lighters in his fist. He lit them and passed one over. Before I knew it I had the thing between my lips. I thought, I shouldn't be doing this. Anyway, I thought, I might as well smoke the damn thing but with the resolution that this would really be my last cigarette.

'When I came home at teatime I confessed. I said to Sue, "I have had a smoke today," and I explained the tale. She was very upset, very disappointed. From that day to this, I've never had a cigarette. Even when I've been knocking the ale down, I've never really had the urge to join in the smoking. In fact on one of the No Smoking Days I was invited to a do at the local hospital as a prime example of a hopeless case who succeeded in giving up.

'I think I am a slightly reformed character from what I used to be, though I do still have too much pop occasionally.'

Fred and Sue's first child was born in the autumn of 1987 and named Jack in honour of Sue's father and Fred's profession. He was christened by an old friend and customer, the Reverend Barry Newth, at his church in the Yorkshire Dales parish of Kirkby Malham. It was a trade in kind for which Fred paid by making a weathercock for the church.

Roger was born in the summer of 1991. Fred was then fifty-three.

Sue had got used to people inquiring if Fred was her father. Among other parents at nursery, and then at school, Fred was taken for the boys' grandfather.

'It doesn't bother me at all,' he said, wheeling Roger to the nursery. 'It demonstrates I'm still in good condition, still of a good breeding quality. I think it's right to say you're as old as you feel. I feel twenty-odd.'

Fred's first brood were girls. He had no advance preference for boys but was pleased to find them more ready to take an interest in the essential things of life, steam engines and chimneys. Jack could name steam engine parts before he could walk properly. Roger learned to peep like a steam engine whistle while he was still being fed from the spoon.

Jack started to go out to the engine shed to 'work' with Fred. 'He's a nuisance,' Fred said, enjoying his company. 'if I put a spanner down it disappears. But he has an encyclopaedic memory. If you ask him where it is a week later he'll go and find it straight away. He has one bad fault though, he goes round digging holes, especially when it's raining. There's holes everywhere full of water. I think he's a frustrated coal miner.

'I don't actually prefer boys to girls – I like both – but I've more time to give them attention now than I had with the earlier brood. I was too busy earning a living. It was hard work sometimes paying the rent and keeping them fed and in clothes. With television and what's sprung from it, I earn money easier now than I did twenty years ago. And I think as you get older you become more patient.'

Fred had certainly become more patient with noise. With a few years' interval of quietness, he had swapped the pop music of teenagers for the racket of young children. 'I think he now understands that noise is just other people enjoying themselves,' Sue said. 'And it might have helped that he's more deaf than he used to be.'

At the beginning the age difference between them used to make Fred worry that she might leave him for somebody, as he said, 'younger and more handsome'. Time and her reassurance had put that fear to rest. But another effect of age difference needed more getting over. The world in which she grew up in the 1960s was very different from Fred's world of the 1940s. She is a child of her time, liberal, assertive, given to negotiation. Fred is a child of his time but a spiritual inhabitant of the more distant days of a hundred years ago, as Sue recognized from the beginning:

'I realized that he had an awful lot of Victorian values, particularly in his attitudes to the woman's role. He thought it was the woman's job to stay at home and do the washing and cook the tea while the man went out to earn the bread. But I think that sort of edge has gone off him and he realizes that the modern world is changing and he'll have to change a little bit with it.

'He has succumbed a bit to domesticity. He likes vacuuming and makes a much better job than I do. He's a perfectionist and gets into all the corners. He's a good fire lighter. He cleans the windows, which he's always done, because he likes to see them twinkly bright. He lights the fires and polishes the brasses.

'I wouldn't ask him to do jobs beyond his competence. I wouldn't ask him to do the washing because he'd put in everything in one load and Roger's beautiful white baby things would come out stained from Fred's working overalls. Nor would I ask him to do the ironing, again partly because of his perfectionism. He'd take so long over one garment that we'd all be wearing crumpled clothes waiting for him to get on with it.

'I think you've got to strike a balance. You can't divide all the jobs fifty-fifty. I've mentioned things I wouldn't expect him to do. And I wouldn't expect him to ask me to go up and renovate the 1854 chimney he's built on our house top or to carry on with riveting the fire box of his steam engine. He helps me with some things in the house and I take an interest and help him as far as I can in his engine shed. We can't divide it fifty-fifty. I think housework is divided ninety per cent me, ten per cent Fred.

'A few years ago, before I was married, I would have expected my husband to do a lot more than Fred does in the house, but I've had to modify my values just as Fred has modified his. I'd always thought that I'd return to work after I'd had my children. If we both worked in offices I suppose I would have done, but it's just not practical with our lifestyle. Fred comes home cold and wet from grafting all day. Sometimes he'll have busted his thumb, hit it with a hammer, and you couldn't expect him to come and start doing things in the house. It just wouldn't be fair.

'I might have got through a good amount of work at home, housework, children, the office work for the business, but that's nothing like working out in the wind and rain. It wouldn't be reasonable to expect him to start again once he came in at teatime. I want him to come in and relax or to go across to his workshop and do something that interests him. I take time out to do the things I enjoy during the day and he should be able to do what he wants in the evening.

'What I do find a bit hard to bear is that he'll always favour a job he wants to do in the workshop above one I want done in the house. The stairs are nearly derelict. I have to make do with a kitchen like a ship's galley three feet wide. It's an example of his perfectionism. He won't start until he can make a super-duper job. The shell of the house extension. where I've been promised a new kitchen on the ground floor, was finished a long time ago. He just won't get on with fitting it out. In the meantime he's using it as a place to keep the new wheels he's made for his traction engine.

'The effect of all this is that we still divide our money-earning in a fairly conventional way. Fred goes out to work and I look after the paperwork. I'm in charge of finance, all the bookkeeping and the household expenses as well. I decide which of the invitations for after-dinner speeches we accept. I don't want anything that'd make Fred look cheap or silly. I don't take on sportsmen's dinners because they want fast, vulgar jokes, which isn't Fred's line at all.'

A NEW lifestyle evolved naturally from their circumstances and different talents. Fred accepted the changes without demur and buckled down cheerfully to his allotted domestic tasks. It became clear, however, that he had in no way abandoned his old-fashioned outlook.

'I've been in the army, you know, and I've always been good under orders. It's discipline, you see, which we could all do with more of In my first marriage I wasn't ordered to do anything. I just did what I wanted, which I suppose is a bit selfish. Now I've got to fall in line a bit more or I get a telling off. I actually do the washing up sometimes. I've become quite proficient at it. It's one way to keep my fingernails clean.

'Sue's certainly smartened me up. I've got a more upmarket wardrobe than I used to have, things for leisure. She's talked me into wearing shoes instead of boots except for work. Instead of one suit and a waistcoat I've now got a grand selection of pullovers and cardigans and two pairs of shoes in fact. I've had to abandon my thick woolly grey socks in favour of lots of pairs of fine black ones. I now have a whole variety of caps for doing different things in, posh ones for appearing in public and my old oily ones for work.

'I have a wash more often than I used to. I have a shower every night, though it's fair to say I couldn't have done that until fairly recently when I completed our splendid new bathroom on the upper floor of the new extension I've built.

'Another thing, I'm not allowed to read the evening paper at the tea table, which is a bit annoying because the six o'clock news is on the radio and television at the same time and I miss that. I'm not keeping abreast of what's happening as I should. But that's a minor drawback. She's not all that bad. She's all right.

'I don't think there's any way now of complete escape from feminist ideas of equal rights and all of that. It's been helped by the virtual disappearance of heavy manual jobs. There are not many jobs left now that need strength. I saw a woman driving a truck the other day and we have a woman friend who has put in for a heavy goods licence. But even truck driving is no longer heavy work. A great Volvo tractor unit is lighter to handle and runs more smoothly than my old Landrover. But there is a young lady, I believe, working as a steeplejack in Manchester and that can't be made light work. It's barely changed in essentials from a hundred years ago.

'Basically I'm still a Victorian at heart. When you look at the mess we're in, who could deny that they were right and we've gone wrong? There was a much bigger proportion of men working hard for a living than there are now. The lady's place was to be at home getting the tea ready. Half of the buggers when they come home now have to set to and make their own tea. "I've just got back from the office, darling. Your tea's in the oven. I'm going out to the bingo."

'It's a weird situation these days in many homes and in the country at large. It's like the last days of the Roman empire after they'd retreated back to Rome from what had been a huge empire. Half of them turned homosexual, went queer, and nearly all of them relapsed into endless pleasure seeking. They'd taught the world to build roads and aqueducts, to sink baths and install underfloor heating, to regulate life by law. Then they all went bad. Their descendants make racing cars and washing machines. It's the end of the road.

'All empires have their great days and pass. The ancient Egyptians built the pyramids but they were reduced afterwards to racing about on camels. I think we've had our day too. I don't want to seem like a diehard but if you think about England's great days; the invention and perfecting of the steam engine and industrial machinery in the late eighteenth and early nineteenth century, the canals and coal mines and factories, the zeal and the optimism, the empire that, even when I was a child, spanned the world; when you think of that and what we've come to in our national and personal life, it can only be seen as a terminal decline. From about 1790 to about 1914 we led the world. Since then in almost every way we've been running down hill.'

DOWN THE WELL

'I'm now in my mid-fifties, at an age when people are beginning to ask how much longer I'm going to climb chimneys. Often there's an implication that by the law of averages my luck one day must run out.

'I've had frights enough up chimneys but never any deep apprehension that I'm going to fall off. The only nasty fall I've ever had was in one of the children's bedrooms, that time. I landed on a drilling machine, knocked myself unconscious and damaged my ribs.

'You never know what fate has in store. I remember an old friend who had just retired. He came from a family of steeplejacks and worked up chimneys himself from the time he left school. "I've got through," he said. "and now I'm going to enjoy having things safe and easy."

'A few days later he was knocked down and killed by a lorry loaded with lettuces for market.

'We all fear different things and we're all vulnerable to different dangers. One of the jobs that caused me most apprehension was shovelling earth. It was on an island in a lake in the Irwell valley. Industrial dereliction had been cleared up and there was now this pleasant lake with its island and wooded shores. The authorities wished to make it something of a bird sanctuary and they were anxious in doing the work to attract more birds, not to frighten off the birds that were already there. They came for me because I enjoy a reputation, except perhaps among some neighbours, for doing jobs quietly.

'The island rose precipitously out of the lake. The plan was to shovel earth from the top over the cliff edge so as to form a gently shelving beach to make it easy for wading birds to come ashore. A mechanical digger would have done the job in no time but it would have been expensive and difficult to get it out to the island and the noise would have scared the birds away. It had to be a shovel job. It wasn't really my line but it could be started in the week between Christmas and New Year which is a doldrum time for getting jobs done with everybody everywhere taking their prolonged winter break. We took it on.

'The council boatman landed Donald and me on the less steep side of the island with our digging tools. He left us a couple of lifejackets. There were jokes about not falling in. But when we got to the edge of the cliff it didn't seem so funny. It was a sheer drop into deep water, and I can't swim. I tried wearing the lifejacket but it was too hot and cumbersome to work in, so from there on I was dicing with death. We shovelled away, at first making no impression at all, but gradually the beach began to form under shallow water and eventually broke the surface.

'I believe it has been quite successful in attracting wading birds. I'm glad to have done my bit for the birds and the environment. But it's the last time. I'll stick to the safety of chimneys.

'The nearest brush I've had with death came again through not sticking to chimneys. It was down a well in the grounds of a beautiful farmhouse up on the moors near Rivington Pike where a friend of mine lived. All that was to be seen were two big flat flagstones, about eight feet by four which sealed the well at ground level. One of the flagstones was cracked.

'To give us an idea what might be below, my friend rolled up his *Financial Times*, put a light to it and shoved it through the crack. Squinting through, we watched it fall down the shaft, turning over in an airless sort of void. It came to rest on a dry surface about forty feet down.

'I wondered whether it might have been the shaft for an old colliery. Years ago there were quite a few in that area.

Whatever it was, my friend wanted the well cover made safe to carry weight. It was in fact part of the yard where cars were regularly driven and he owned a big traction engine which had to pass quite close.

'So one Monday morning, when it was too bitterly cold to proceed with a hospital pointing job we had on the go, we went up to the farm to have a proper look. We crowbarred the flagstones up and moved them away on rollers. The shaft was about five feet in diameter and lined for the top fifteen feet or so with small Georgian bricks. They had been laid dry, without mortar, which was a common practice in well building. Their foundation was solid rock, but it had been hacked into a crude sort of circle which had been made good, after a fashion, by laying baulks of timber across the irregular spots. Most of this timber had now rotted away. The part of the brickwork that had been laid directly on rock seemed all right but the part laid on the timber baulks now had no foundation. Some of the bricks had fallen; others stayed there only by long habit. It all looked rather unhealthy and dangerous.

'We set about it cautiously. We put two scaffolding poles across the top and I went down in my bosun's chair to take a close look at the brickwork. I thought it could be repaired. We could undermine the bad areas, put in a proper footing based on the rock and rebuild on that.

'We built a working platform of strong scaffolding poles fifteen feet down with an access ladder from the top. I went to work. In place of the rotted timber, I put in a solid stone footing, made from old window bottoms from demolished houses, with the intention that the job shouldn't have to be done again in another two hundred years. I patched it up with a dozen bricks there, a dozen over here and a few more there.

'It was beginning to look firm and secure and, by way of diversion, I decided to see what was at the bottom of the shaft. If it had once been a mine there might be some interesting galleries leading off from the shaft. I told Donald what I was doing and lowered myself down in my bosun's chair. I was cautious about alighting, which was just as well. What I'd taken for the bottom of the shaft was actually a rotted wooden platform, built perhaps to stop muck falling down or to facilitate changing the pump rods. Dangling in my bosun's chair and poking about in the rubbish I came across objects somebody must have lost long ago, a knife with a bone handle and an umbrella with a fancy knob. I was prodding to see what else there might be when Donald's alarmed voice came echoing down: "You'd better come up, Fred. There's muck running from behind the brickwork." Within seconds a small shower of grit struck me. Bigger lumps followed. With the system of pulleys we use for the bosun's chair a man can haul himself up, though slowly. It wasn't slowly that day. I don't think anybody ever went up quicker in a bosun's chair.

'We stood at the top, weighing it up. But nothing more happened. It looked like a small temporary disturbance. I descended the fifteen feet back down the ladder to my working platform and Donald went for another load of bricks. While I was waiting I spotted an old brick that would have to come out. I tapped it with my brick hammer and out it flirted. I knew immediately something fearful was going to happen. There was a horrible seething noise. The whole wall of bricks groaned. It's strange how the mind works in an emergency. I remember calmly thinking, "I mustn't leave my trowel and spirit level down here." I hurled them beyond the crumbling rim above and shot up the ladder after them. The next second everything started to slide down the shaft. The whole wall, all the way round, disintegrated. The brickwork went rumbling down and behind it tons of earth and stones from beneath the surrounding tarmac. Everything was sucked down as though into a giant funnel.

'When I returned, some considerable time later, to a state of relative calm I figured out what had happened. Apart from having lost its foundations in places, the wall, lacking mortar, was no more than a pile of bricks in circular form. The bricks should really have been pressed more tightly one against the other which would have given the wall the strength of an arch. Then, the old timers who built it had filled in behind the wall with chippings of stone which, when the earth settled, was exerting terrific pressure on this cylinder of brickwork. But it had been like that for years and I don't think it would have collapsed if I hadn't knocked out that one fatal brick. The surrounding stones and earth broke through at the weakened place and brought everything cascading down.

'My working platform fifteen feet down was smashed to pieces and its strong scaffolding poles bent like paper clips. The two pipes we'd placed across the well to enable me to make my first inspection descent on the bosun's chair were drawn forty feet down before jamming themselves between the rock walls of the lower part of the shaft. And we saw something else. The wooden platform, where I'd found the knife and the umbrella had completely gone. Everything had disappeared into deep black water which we could now see more than a hundred feet down. That was a real shaker. As I mentioned, I can't swim. Even if I'd survived the avalanche I wouldn't have survived the water.

'It gave us a hollow feeling to have to start work again there, but then we saw the landslide had made such a thorough job of cleaning the shaft that we could make a completely new start, which is always preferable to patching. We used about five thousand new bricks and left a nice solid circular wall that should last forever. Then, addressing the job we'd originally been engaged to do, we made sure it'd be safe for vehicles to cross. We fitted two big iron girders across the top, capable of taking the weight of a Centurion tank, and replaced the flagstones on top of them. To the eye it looked no different from the day we first arrived. Nobody could tell we'd been there. But it's a visit I shan't forget. Sometimes, for no apparent reason, I have a sudden vivid recollection of that wall disintegrating into the rumbling darkness below.

'More recently I nearly came to grief in my own backyard. My house is approached from the side down a steep drive which itself runs along the top of a precipitous wooded slope. One night a friend had dropped me at the top of the drive. I'd had a pint or two and didn't feel quite capable of making it down to the house, so I stopped for a pee down into the wood. I must have lost my balance and slipped over the edge. I found myself rolling down between the trees. I was curled up like a hedgehog, seeing the moon and the stars turning above the branches at every revolution.

'The slope is about one in two, fifty per cent as they now say. I was really bouncing. I thought, "If I hit a tree straight on, I'm a goner."

I did actually bring up against an ash tree but something must have cushioned the impact. I got warily to my feet. I'd no nasty pains, no broken bones. But then I had to get back up the hill which is of soft crumbly soil and leaf mould. I was like the proverbial spider in the bath tub, up so far then, whoosh, back to the bottom again.

'Eventually I crawled back to the drive and summoned up the courage to go and face the wife. She was especially cross that I'd lost my new glasses. Sent back to search for them the next day, I was stung by a wasp.

'If I'd been less lucky in my fall, and the worst had come to the worst, Bill Greenhalgh, a friend of mine, might have been able to try out a piece of apparatus he says he's designed for dispatching the departed from the top of our drive direct to the cemetery. A wire hawser would be secured to a tree at this end and run down through the wood and across the river to the cemetery on the far bank. I'd be placed in a coffin resembling a large aluminium cigar case and at the appropriate moment in the funeral service a string would be pulled, like launching a ship, and I'd fire off down the wire and land in the grave on the other side.

'I hope, if it comes to that, everybody will stay around and have a good party afterwards.

'The most shocking accident I ever had was to be laid low by my cap.

'I've got more than one now for different occasions since I've been reformed, but I've always felt affection for my oily working cap. It has a smell all its own. It's so impregnated with oil that people in pubs ask me, "What's the flashpoint of your cap?"

'I've frequently had it on fire, usually when I'm blacksmithing and at the need of the moment I grab it off to get hold of hot iron. Practically, it's there to keep the rain off my head, but it has a big psychological value. It makes me look a few years younger by covering my pale bald head. Without my cap I feel strange, as though somebody's shaved off the top of my head. It's a replacement for hair.

'I wear it indoors and outdoors. Sometimes, when I've come back inebriated after a day out with my steamroller, I've ended up asleep in bed with my cap on.

'It was therefore a very nasty shock when my cap laid me low, a bit like being rounded on by a favourite dog. I was with Susie in the building society withdrawing £2,000 to pay the income tax. I don't know whether it was the stress of having to get the money out or what, but I came over faint and very hot and flustered. I thought I was going to fall on the floor. Susie said I was worrying too much about the money. But it wasn't that. I came home, had a stiff whisky and went to bed. I was going worse. Red blotches were appearing all over the top of my bald head. Sue sent for the doctor. He immediately knew what was wrong – scapho capieitis or something like that. He said I must have caught it from my cap.

'I remembered then that when I was up the ladders a day or two previously my cap had blown off and landed in a puddle on the roof of a spinning mill. The puddle was full of dead pigeons and all sorts of horrible stuff I wrung my cap out and put it back on and by dinner time it was dry. I'd forgotten all about it.

'The doctor thought that some sort of germ from my cap had got into a scratch on top of my head and worked its way underneath the skin. It could be serious. Apparently if it gets round to your eye sockets you could lose your sight.

'It didn't come to that. He gave me some potions and medicines that stopped it spreading and cleared it up, though I felt a bit groggy for a few days afterwards.

'It was an alarming experience. But I still prefer my old cap.'

NEW HORIZONS

IN RECENT years Fred has been working further from home. For most of his life he seldom travelled too far to return in the evening. But now as chimneys get fewer he has to go further afield for good jobs.

It's not an entirely welcome development. Travelling is slow in the Landrover with the ladders and the tackle on the back and driving motor vehicles, apart from his old AJS motorbike, has never been a pleasure. Motorways are a bore, country roads downright dangerous.

'In a steam engine, that many of the country roads were designed for, you can see over the top of the big hedges. Down in a car or Landrover you're half blind. I'm surprised more people don't get killed on country roads. There are a lot of nasty dangerous bends. I suppose they're there because landowners in the past must have been dead awkward and made the road builders go round their fields.'

Nor does Fred find much pleasure in nature. 'There's not much variety to brighten a slow journey. You long for the towns were there's something interesting to see round every corner.'

The travelling hasn't come at the best time of life with Fred in his mid-fifties and with two young children at home. But the distant jobs he is offered – thanks as he says to his 'notoriety' – invariably pay well:

'Perhaps the competition is stiffer round home, where there was once an enormous forest of chimneys and where steeplejacks are still thicker on the ground (or, should I say, in the air?), than elsewhere. If I give an estimate for a job in Bolton some guy can come from Manchester and offer to do it for half the price, whereas at the other end of England they'll pay you a fortune, presumably because other people are asking a lot more. I think also reputation increases with distance, so they'll send for somebody from miles away when there are men on the doorstep capable of doing as good a job. Perhaps that's why the nation is racing up and down the motorways, everybody doing jobs in each other's territory.

'As places to stay, I much prefer pubs to bed and breakfast places, not because the food's necessarily better but because the inmates are more constant. In the B and Bs they change every day and a lot of them are shy and in a highly nervous state, whereas in pubs the regulars keep turning up and at the end of a week or two you know practically all the village, except perhaps the teetotallers.

'I've heard it said that there's a vast difference between people in the north of England and the South, that people in the North are much more friendly. I haven't found that to be true. Most people anywhere are pleasant if you're agreeable with them and equally I suppose everywhere has its quota of awkward buggers.

'Sometimes, on the bigger jobs, I'm booked into quite posh hotels. It took me some time to overcome my fear of them. Until recent years I'd seldom stayed away from home, except in the living van of the steamroller, and I was somewhat overawed by grand hotels. At first it was a bit of an ordeal to go creeping down to breakfast with everybody sitting there frosty-faced. I found the communal eating business frightening, worrying about not picking up the right knife and fork while being gazed at by strange eyes. Then the bill bothered me, even though I wasn't paying it. I wondered however much it was going to amount to after I'd lost count of all the dinners I'd eaten. In one place the guy behind the bar kept saying, "Have another on the room number," and I kept thinking all the time, "That's adding more and more to the amount the people we're working for are going to have to pay."

'You come across a lot of freeloaders in hotels, battening on expenses.

'I used to think you had to be very rich to stay in an hotel. but I know now that most of the people there are on company expenses. Some of them put on airs and graces to appear a bit upmarket but really they're just ordinary people like me, there to earn a living. Since I got over my apprehension I've been quite happy in hotels. I've enjoyed meeting a whole variety of interesting characters I wouldn't have come across in my ordinary routine.

'Sometimes I get homesick. I was once away for a month. It was like being a sailor coming home from the sea. It's late in life to start this new style after coming home for my tea at five o'clock for years and years. I do worry about how Susie is managing with the children on her own and I get frustrated at sitting around in the evening when I could be making a bit of progress with work on my tractor. Then when I do get back I'm a bit hesitant to zoom off into the engine shed in case I get a good talking to from Susie. "You've been away all week and now you've disappeared into the bloody shed" sort of thing. Which is very understandable in a way.'

HOWEVER FAR Fred travels there are fewer chimneys and churches to work on and as the years go by it gets further to the top of those that are left. Fred hums as he climbs, like a model driven by an electric motor, breaking off between numbers to mutter comments and exhortations: 'Come on, Fred, keep going', 'Cold up here this morning' and, increasingly, 'I'm getting too old for this'.

He doesn't mean it, but with the need to go on earning a family income for a further fifteen years or so, he's been working up some new lines that could be carried on in his more mature years.

'I've made quite a lot of weathercocks of late. It isn't exactly a new line. As I mentioned, I made my first when I was in the army, the one cut out from an aluminium tray, which I hoisted up as an embellishment on the roof of the officers' hound kennels. Over the years I've done quite a few for consecrated buildings after my early success at repairing and gilding the weather vanes on Bolton parish church. The most ambitious early one wasn't a cock. We offered to do Gabriel blowing his horn for a village church four miles down the road. The vicar was very keen. The parochial church council gave its approval.

'The procedure is to nip off to the scrapyard and find a piece of copper, then back home to design the thing on paper and then get to work with the fret saw and the big files. I then get the central pivot sorted out and take the whole assembly for the vicar to approve. Then back to stick the gold leaf on, then out again to the church where we usually hoist it to the top of the flagpole with ropes and pulleys.

'Everybody was very pleased with Gabriel, an angel in graceful flight, holding to his lips the mouthpiece of a long slender horn. It turned out to be too slender. The horn broke off, leaving him holding a stump to his mouth. For twenty years he revolved with the wind and sparkled in the sun, looking as though he were smoking a cigar. We'd gone there originally to replace the rotted flagpole. In twenty years the new one had rotted, so in replacing that we brought Gabriel down and fettled him good as new and a fair bit stronger.

'The one I made more recently, for the vicar of Kirkby Malham, the Reverend Barry Newth, also had a rough passage. As has been mentioned, it was done as part of a deal. He wanted a weathercock. I said, "Right, I'll make you a weathercock if you'll christen t' little lad in your 800-year-old font." He did it in a very gracious way and I was anxious that he should be equally pleased with my job for him. So I was upset when he rang me up and reported that heavy winds had brought the weathercock down. I was relieved to find that it wasn't my fault. The flagpole is one of those modern fibreglass jobs, supposed to be very tough but not strong enough, as it turned out, to hold the spindle in high winds. The spindle broke free and the whole assembly came down. Fortunately it landed in a snowdrift and the cock wasn't even dented, so it was fit to go back and I hope I've left it secure against the winds that howl through the Dales.

'We had an unforeseeable bit of bad luck when we first fixed it. Digging in the graveyard for an earthing strip for the lightning conductor we found we were digging up somebody's bones. Whose they were, there's no means of knowing, but they'd been there a long time. Oliver Cromwell had visited the place and the church had been there for ages before him. We buried them all nearly alongside the copper cable, but I believe there had to be a reinternment ceremony.'

ANOTHER LINE Fred hopes to develop is doing up other people's steam engines. Over the years spent in restoring his own engines he has got together all the tools for the job assembled in his backyard workshop, and painfully he has gained experience of disappearing arts and skills. His first big paid-for restoration job was on a stationary steam engine at an estate near Caernarvon, which hadn't run since 1931: 'Vandals had been at it and stripped off the brass bits. The flywheel and the connecting rod lay in the bottom all seized up, red with rust and corroded. Everything was covered in mountains of pigeon droppings and plaster fallen from the engine house walls and ceilings. It was a daunting challenge but it was also a chance to show what I could do.'

Working with Neil Carney, his new and mechanically skilled assistant, Fred restored the engine and the boiler house – 'as good as it was in 1854 when it was first installed, perhaps a bit better.'

He enjoyed the work. His family came down for several weeks during the summer. They stayed in a pleasant pub. The beach was handy and the sun shone. Fred announced to all who might be interested that he was ready for more. What came his way exceeded his wildest ambitions, the magnificent giant of the road, Atlas, a Fowler B6 tractor of 16 1/2 tons, which in its time had hauled trains of heavily loaded trailers the length and breadth of the country. A picture of it had, for a long time, shared pride of place on Fred's parlour wall with the picture of his grandfather Travis in athlete's kit surrounded by his trophies.

Fred had made the acquaintance of the tractor itself and of its owner, James Hervey-Bathurst, of Eastnor Castle, Herefordshire, at a steam rally at Upton-upon-Severn. It was a miserable drizzling day, but a high spot in Fred's memory because James invited him up to the footplate and offered him a drive up and down the sodden field. The sheer speed of the thing, squelching along at eighteen miles an hour, left Fred drained.

Atlas needs two on the footplate, a driver and a steersman, and the following year James invited Fred to share the trip with him from Eastnor to Upton. It's not a long trip for a vehicle of Atlas's pace but it took a long time on account of the frequent stops for refreshment. James was impressed with Fred's soundness as a steam engine man. He gave him the job of having new main bearings made and fitting them.

It was too tight a squeeze to work on Atlas in Fred's backyard. He got the use of floor space and an overhead crane in an engineering works. Restored and revived, Atlas came rattling out on its test run through the streets of Bolton. It was a wild day. The wind blew the smoke horizontally past the upper windows of terraced houses and tore at the crew on Atlas's footplate. They clung on, looking more like a pirate crew than traction engine drivers. At every traffic light people climbed aboard and others bailed out. Half of Bolton must have done some distance on Atlas. Fred enjoined them all to hearken to the silence of the bearings. He felt the metal around the crank and announced that it was uniformly warm.

Delivering Atlas to the courtyard of Eastnor Castle, Fred was accompanied on the footplate by Bill Walker, who looks after James Hervey-Bathurst's collection of steam vehicles. James and his dog were waiting for them in front of the main door.

Fred got down and, never one to understate a drama, gave a graphic description of the wild storm through which they'd driven. 'We did twenty-nine miles, with drops of rain on top of the oil on top of the bearings, so that must mean it's running right.'

'Quite cool?' James asked.

'Uniformly hot,' Fred replied.

'Sounds great. Can we hear it running?'

Bill Walker restarted the engine.

James listened, keenly at first, and then with growing pleasure. 'Fantastic job.'

'I'm quite happy with it myself,' Fred confessed.

Later, surveying the lake and woods and hills of James's estate from the battlements, Fred asked him how he'd come to be interested in steam engines.

James thought it was in his blood. 'When my grandfather was in the Grenadier Guards on the way to Omdurman the train came to a stop in Egypt. I think the footplate crew knew what they were heading for and let the fire go down. My grandfather got it going again and set the train under way. He was mentioned in the regimental history for that. Then he drove a shunter in Southampton docks at the general strike.'

'It's definitely in your blood,' Fred said.

'Then when we came to repair the estate roads with stone from the quarry we used to have, we bought a steamroller. Then we bought a traction engine in Ireland, which we used for threshing, then I bought a Foden steam lorry which was derelict and spent a lot of time doing it up.

'My mother was very keen that I should get married. She thought there was no chance of that until the steam lorry was finished so she used to come down at weekends to help me paint it. When we finished it I did get married.'

Fred thought that quite reasonable. In the light of his own experience he wondered how James's marriage had survived the years of doing up Atlas from a rusted wreck.

James knew the problem. All too many steam men of his acquaintance had eventually to sell their engines to finance the divorce brought on by their time-consuming and costly repair. 'I'm very keen not to lose Atlas so I keep washing up and looking after the children.'

'I've actually started doing a bit of washing up,' Fred confessed.

'You're lucky,' James said, 'because you haven't got a stately home as well. If you've got a stately home and several engines—'

'That's double trouble,' Fred said.

James said he had a valuable ally in Bill Walker, the tall old character who had been on the footplate with Fred on the delivery journey. He not only looked after James's steam engines but helped with the domestic diplomacy as well. 'As an old steam man he's been through all that kind of trouble, seen it hundreds of times, so every time we're about to go off to a rally he turns up at the house with flowers for my wife, a box of chocolates, Easter eggs for the children.'

'Clever stuff,' Fred said.

'He's quite right. He does the right thing.'

'A bunch of flowers goes a long way,' Fred commented, speaking from hearsay rather than experience.

'It does, especially before a rally.'

Next day they drove Atlas and its train of caravans from the castle to the showground at Upton-upon-Severn. As usual among steam men, they started several hours late, but they made up time on the way. Old Bill went ahead by car and imperiously held up traffic at all the crossroads so they could come hurtling round, cutting back from their eighteen miles an hour down the straights only sufficiently to avoid rolling over.

The journey was done in record time, due partly to Atlas having been brought up to spanking condition, partly to Bill's command of the junctions, and by no means least to their resolution in puffing past all the pubs en route without a single stop.

Neither Fred nor Sue can imagine his retirement from steeplejacking.

Weathercock-making and steam engine-repairing are welcome sidelines but they are perfectionist jobs with a low rate of remuneration reckoned by the hour. The after-dinner speaking and the promotional work came with what Fred calls his 'notoriety' and they could pass with it.

Anyway, they're not enough to make a good life. 'Just to be propped up in front of a camera to represent soap powder or what have you, I think that'd finish me off.'

'He has to climb,' Sue said. 'He's a steeplejack before anything else. That's the main love of his life. He'd be a very, very sad person if ever he had to give it up. He'd be very difficult to live with. He's bad enough if even for a few days he doesn't have a steeplejack job going. He enjoys the solitary life, the king of the castle with only the birds for company. When he's working in good weather up something really high he comes home in the evening thrilled with the view he's enjoyed all day and pleased with the job he's doing. That's his life, that's what he is, a steeplejack.'

'I've got to have the steeplejacking aspect of my life,' Fred agreed. 'Some bits of it are humdrum and some bits unbelievably exciting. I suppose I'll slow down a bit when I'm an old chap but the ideal way out, instead of dying in bed of something horrible, would be just to drop off a chimney some sunny day when I'm about seventy-five.

'And that'll be the end.'

Dibnahisms

I'm just a bum who climbs chimneys.

Height gives you a wonderful feeling of grandeur.
You're the king of the castle up here.

I set out as a steeplejack in my youth to preserve chimneys.
I've finished by knocking most of them down.

One mistake up here, and it's half a day
out with the undertaker.

A man who says he feels no fear is either a fool or a liar.

I realize that steam engines are not everybody's cup of tea.
But they're what made England great.

Steam engines don't answer back.
You can belt them with a hammer and they say nowt.

The modern world stinks.

We've become a nation of con men,
living by selling double glazing to each other.

I'd had a pint or two.

Did you like that?

Picture Credits

BBC Books would like to thank the following for providing photographs and for permission to reproduce copyright material. While every effort has been made to trace and acknowledge all copyright holders, we would like to apologise should there have been any errors or omissions. Abbreviations: *t* top, *b* bottom, *c* centre, *tl* top left, *tr* top right, *bl* bottom left, *br* bottom right.

First Plate Section
Page 1*t* and *b* Fred Dibnah Collection; 2–3*t* Humphrey Spender; 2*b* Arthur Smith; 3*c* Fred Dibnah Collection; 3*b* Arthur Smith; 4 (all) Fred Dibnah Collection; 5*t* Fred Dibnah Collection; 5*bl* and *br* Arthur Smith; 6*t* Arthur Smith; 6*b* David Secombe for the BBC; 7*tl* Fred Dibnah Collection; 7*tr* Humphrey Spender; 7*bl* and *br* Fred Dibnah Collection; 8*t* Tillotsons Newspapers Ltd; 8*c* and *b* Fred Dibnah Collection.

Second Plate Section
1*t* Oldham Chronicle; 1*c* Tillotsons Newspapers Ltd; 1*b* Fred Dibnah Collection; 2*t* Daily Express; 2*b* Sefton Samuels; 3 (all) David Secombe for the BBC; 4*t* Arthur Smith; 4*c* and *b* Fred Dibnah Collection; 5*t* Fred Dibnah Collection; 5*c, bl* and *br* David Secombe for the BBC; 6*t* and *c* David Secombe for the BBC; 6*bl* Fred Dibnah Collection; 6*br* Arthur Smith; 7*t* Arthur Smith; 7*c* Fred Dibnah Collection; 7*b* David Secombe for the BBC; 8 Peter Ainsley.

Index